Co-Crazy

One Psychologist's Recovery from
Codependency and Addiction

*A Memoir and Roadmap
to Freedom*

—m—

By

Sarah Michaud, PsyD

Co-Crazy: One Psychologist's Recovery from Codependency and Addiction,
published December, 2021
Cover Design: Elizabeth Leeper
Interior Design & Layout: Howard Johnson
Editorial & Proofreading: Highline Editorial, New York, NY, Taylor Morris, Katie Barger, Karen Grennan
Photo credits: About the Author Photograph by Isa Rose Photography

 **SDP Publishing**

Published by SDP Publishing, an imprint of SDP Publishing Solutions, LLC.

For more information about this book, contact Lisa Akoury-Ross at SDP Publishing by email at info@SDPPublishing.com.

To obtain permission(s) to use material from this work, please submit a written request to:

SDP Publishing
Permissions Department
PO Box 26
East Bridgewater, MA 02333
or email your request to info@SDPPublishing.com

ISBN-13 (print): 978-1-7367204-3-1
ISBN-13 (ebook): 978-1-7367204-4-8
Library of Congress Control Number: 2021921741

Printed in the United States of America

To all the people who are in recovery, struggling with recovery, who may not know they need recovery, or are otherwise suffering ... and to all the people who love them.

Table of Contents

"You do not fix me. You do not manage me.
That is not love."

—President Fitzgerald to Olivia Pope, television series *Scandal*

Introduction

Healing codependency can be a painful and soul-crushing journey because we are looking at behaviors that we don't even want to admit we are doing. Most of us grew up with some kind of dysfunction. We get our beliefs about ourselves through our interpretations of our world. Interactions we had with our parents and our environment causes us to develop core beliefs about ourselves and our relationships with others. Some of those beliefs can be empowering and build self-esteem. Some can break a spirit.

Growing up in a household with addiction, abuse, mental illness, or any other situation where your parents don't address their own feelings or experiences, creates a person who keeps working out unhealthy patterns repetitively in their relationships to try to gain mastery over these old wounds. We are all trying to recover from our childhoods in one form or another. We try to heal from this brokenness by our relentless preoccupation with others, rather than keeping the focus on ourselves.

This is what I call co-crazy. You feel crazy in a relationship. Trying to fix, change, or save another while your emotional world decompensates.

Even when we realize we can't fix people, we keep trying. Heartbreak, pain, fear, and outrage can bring us to our knees exactly like an addict's substance will do to them. Being in a relationship with an active addict or alcoholic, someone who "drives us crazy," or someone we want to control or change, will block the joy of connectedness that we desire with the ones we love. Control disrupts and destroys anything that is good about the relationship.

Acceptance of powerlessness was the hardest thing for someone like me. It meant that it would no longer help to read more books, try new strategies, manage more, work harder, figure out solutions, or go to more experts. I had already tried all of that. The answer I found was to love myself first and to have the courage to face who I had become. We are the source of our own freedom and happiness. I am the problem.

I know this to be true because I've worked with addicts and codependents for twenty-five years. I am also an addict in long-term recovery. I have loved many sober and not-sober people. I got clean and sober thirty-five years ago, but I have hit many bottoms since then with my codependency. My mother was an alcoholic, my father was an angry codependent, and I married two sober alcoholics. One of my husbands relapsed into active addiction, and I watched my life blow apart. When that happened, there wasn't enough therapy, exercise, or meditation that was going to heal me. No self-help book or seminar would make things better.

The delusion was that if I just focused on the other person and put all my effort into healing them, they would get better and I'd be okay.

This is the big lie.

The reality is that both people will get worse. I've seen how the relentlessness of this perception can destroy people's lives. The person trying to save the other person will end up with anxiety, depression, physical problems, resentment, fear, and shame. The subject of the efforts will get resentful and blame their problems on the person trying to save them. When an addict is ready to change, they will. It isn't about the expensive treatment facility. It isn't about the right medication. It isn't about the timing. It isn't about manipulating them into treatment.

It is about changing the focus.

By reading this book, you will cultivate compassion for yourself. You may even forgive yourself like I had to after I blamed myself for my husband's relapse. We can forgive ourselves for things we have or haven't done, for the behaviors we are ashamed of, for the ways we parented, for the limits we haven't set, for the fear and anger we have taken out on people, for the ways we have tried to control people's lives or even the ways we have shut down completely. There is a new way—a better way—than to continue to struggle with the people we care about.

This book talks about the truth with zero judging or shaming. You will assess your life and your relationships. You didn't know what you didn't know. As you delve deeper into the book, create spaciousness and a new paradigm for your relationship to self—no feeling bad, no self-destruction, no drama, no story, no interpretation or opinions, and no guilt. Let's look at what works and what doesn't, what we need to own or not, and what needs to be healed within ourselves to have powerful, supportive, and spirit-driven relationships.

At its core, this book is about my journey and the tools that helped me find peace and joy. I didn't like some of the suggestions that were made to me, but my despair made me willing, and taking them saved my life. So, you may not like some of the things I have to say, but try to pause and take a breath. The healing from the craziness of loving someone you want to change can feel counterintuitive. This new kind of love is for warriors. As you begin, have courage, trust, a little boldness, and a willingness to not know an outcome.

We work hard, spending more and more time losing ourselves trying to fix the relationship. It doesn't ever work but we keep doing it. Sometimes it is how we relate to people in all our relationships. It feels crazy to try so hard and have situations keep getting worse. At the least, this style of relating creates a lot of drama in your life with no peace. If you want healing and freedom, try some of these suggestions. That is what I want for you—a breath, a bit of comfort, a moment when you can feel ok. It can happen. I promise.

I begin my story with my last crash of co-crazy ten years ago when I discovered my husband had lost his sobriety with a new addiction to opiates. I had prior crashes where I had begun to take a stand but then went right back to lying to myself. Then I'll tell you the story of my addiction and how my own codependency developed. Whether you are an addict or a codependent, you will see that if I can recover and change, anyone can.

I'll describe all the feelings, types of thinking, and subsequent behaviors that make up someone with co-crazy. Scattered throughout the book are tools for you to pick up and begin to apply to your daily life, and also some tips and questions to ask yourself. The *power tools* of recovery are titled *Leaving Crazy Town*. These are the bigger and broader suggestions that create the foundation for your recovery before diving deeper into more specific exercises within each chapter. You get to decide what you are ready for and when you are willing to take action.

I have a simple request of you: try to embrace your recovery with love for yourself, compassion for others, and a good sense of humor. There will be times when everything seems backward and doesn't make sense. This is what the healing from co-crazy feels like. It is difficult to tolerate the unknown, new ideas, and new ways of thinking. You may have intense feelings while you practice these new behaviors. This work requires bravery and an open, vulnerable heart. It is about getting to know ourselves with fierceness and honesty, where the truth is more important than looking good or being right. Your faith in your abilities may have been lost. Let's get it back.

This journey can be liberating yet nauseating, hopeful yet dreadful. You absolutely have the freedom to get your life back, but you need to see love differently. Loving someone is not taking care of them in a way that includes perpetually sacrificing yourself. Real warrior love is about risking telling the truth, setting boundaries, being your true self, processing your own feelings, not blaming, and letting go of an outcome you think you want. It is loving ourselves first and allowing someone else to follow their own path, even if that path is disturbing or doesn't match your vision for their life. Ultimately, it is about having peace within our bodies and hearts, not the restless need to escape.

I will never forget a suggestion I read in a parenting book back when my son was young. It implied that if I kept packing my son's backpack, he would begin to think he couldn't do it. We lose our own power, energy, self-love, serenity, and peace while we focus on another, but we take away these things from them as well. If you've been this co-crazy person, remember: no blame, no self-hate, no screaming, and no regrets.

A fair warning: there are plenty of unvarnished and gloves-off words in this book. It's because in many circumstances this comes down to life or death for both people. Note to readers: I use the word addict to mean anyone addicted to drugs, alcohol, or anything else they have an addictive relationship to. I also realize some are sensitive to the word crazy when it comes to women and mental health. This is meant to describe the way I and many others have felt when we are involved in painful relationships; it is not meant to offend anyone. Lastly, both men and women can be co-crazy, but often women seek out help more frequently than men. This book can be helpful to both, but I refer mainly to women in my writing.

Let's just look at the facts: My son can pack his own back-pack. I couldn't save my mother from her drinking. I couldn't save my father from his rage. I couldn't save my husband from his addiction. They were responsible for their own lives. You may be avoiding yours.

Welcome to your life and mine.

A CRAZY AND CO-CRAZY LIFE: Crash and Burn

We don't reach the mountaintop
from the mountaintop.
We start at the bottom and
climb up.
Blood is involved.

—Cheryl Strayed, *Brave Enough*

1

The Co-Crazy
in All of Us

The summer between my first and second year of a doctorate program, I ended up in a treatment facility. It wasn't due to a relapse. It was because I couldn't stop certain behaviors. I felt lost, confused, angry, detached, and resigned because I thought that I may never understand the reason for my continuous train of unsuccessful relationships.

On the first day in a group on relationship dynamics within families with addiction/dysfunction, the leader wrote on the board:

Addicts: 95 percent pain and problems, 5 percent addiction.
Co-addicts: 100 percent pain and problems.

If we have an addiction, love someone with an addiction, or are driven by an unconscious drive for approval or love, we all have our own brokenness. We may use a particular thing to escape or utilize other defenses to cope with our past pain and present struggles. We may not all suffer the severe consequences that addiction causes, but we have all felt hurt, upset, angry, lost, ashamed, betrayed, fearful, or alone. The human condition is about trying to learn to navigate this world in a way that works without getting lost in the old patterns of relating that lead to chronic frustration and repetitive loss.

The main components of co-crazy are lack of relationship to self, a preoccupation with others, and being driven by other people's opinions of us. Living by the belief that "if I fix them, I will be okay" drives us to continuously compromise ourselves to be loved and try to manage the lives of others while we ignore our own. There is no sense of solid ground because it is based on how someone else feels, and this is always changing. The result is chronic low-level anxiety and a persistent, invisible, gripping tension in the body as we fight our powerlessness over others, forever looking outside ourselves to understand who we are.

It does not have to be a relationship with a spouse. You could be taking care of a son who is forty-years-old and still living in your basement. He's depressed and drinking Budweisers while you are upstairs spending all your time worrying. Maybe it's your mother or grandmother who drives you crazy because you let them run your life, afraid to speak up and be yourself. Perhaps you have some people in your life who don't treat you well but you can't let them go. Co-crazy is everywhere. For years, I've run into people who are unhappy because of someone else's behavior. We give our power and self-esteem to another, waiting and wanting them to change so we can feel better. It doesn't work.

We are all co-crazy to a certain extent. Co-crazy is about ways of thinking, how we deal with feelings, and participation in behaviors we use to avoid our internal states. It's a perfect description of the lengths people will go to cope with their pain or to try to change another person. It doesn't matter whether you're highly educated or not, rich or poor, successful or not, or a kind, decent, thoughtful person who likes to help—none of this matters when your thinking is backward, and you are focused outward rather than inward. Being driven by our inability to tol-erate our feelings leads us to believe we have the power to change another. This recovery is not something you will figure out with your mind because everything about changing co-crazy behav-iors is counterintuitive. It doesn't feel right at first. You'll have to begin to act differently in order to stop being in pain.

Let's tally up the many things we have tried that didn't work. A client of mine once brought in a long list of all the specific things she had done to help her drug-addicted daughter over a ten-year period. There were doctors' names, appointments made, treatment centers arranged, jobs suggested, medications recommended, and money managing techniques she shared. It added up to about thirty items. Her daughter had not followed up on any of them. In another column were five action items that her daughter had completed. They were her own ideas.

Part of being human is we want things to go our way. We want people to behave the way we want them to. We do not want our loved ones to suffer and feel pain. This is normal. Co-crazy is on a continuum. At one end could be a new mom who, due to her anxiety and fear about parenting, becomes a bit controlling with her child. The other extreme could be a couple who has re-mortgaged their home three times to pay for another treatment center for their son's addiction. Where you are on the scale depends on how much you are presently suffering and how deeply attached you are to what the other is doing.

When clients' lives were getting colorful due to trying to save or change someone, it was both fascinating and infuriating to witness their lack of willingness to see their part in the problem. It was shocking, yet understandable, to hear their resistance and witness their participation in the co-crazy dance. The suggestion that they may need to look at their behaviors was frequently met with a scowl, anger, or lengthy explanations as to why their situation was different. It was terrifying for them to feel the fear of not having control over the outcome of their loved one's actions. The lie is "the more involved I am in their lives, the more control I can now have over what happens to them." Nope.

All these stories began to upset me, most likely because I was going through the same thing in my life. I saw the wasted time of obsessing about something you cannot change. What bothered me was the denial, and I would often say to clients, "You want your son to go to AA, but don't you think you need Al-Anon? How is it different?" I was trying to process my situation in my marriage while counseling folks about their co-crazy behaviors. Listening to someone in denial can be frustrating but slamming someone with the truth doesn't work either. It is a painful process to wake up to the fact that you are powerless, and the solution is to own your part. Damn.

It was clear to me that most people had trouble with taking care of themselves in a relationship—whether it was speaking their truth, setting boundaries, leaving a relationship, asking for their needs to be met, or expressing their feelings. I saw early maladaptive coping skills still operating even though they didn't need them anymore. For example, a woman in her fifties was still not able to say "No" to her mother, even though she wasn't relying on her now for food and shelter. Intellectually, she knew she was safe. However, emotionally she still felt like she couldn't upset her mother because it felt too dangerous.

After years of seeing people in my practice, it became more transparent that underneath many addictions was the unhealed co-crazy. The pain from childhood was still playing out in people's lives with their addictions masking it.

When I crashed and burned from using substances, I needed to learn how to relate to others without using my old tools of people-pleasing, manipulation, avoidance, rationalization, seduction, or not telling the whole truth. My belief was that I needed to present a certain way so you would like me. I wanted authentic relationships, but I didn't know how to be myself. We all want connection but how can we have a connection *and* be ourselves? When we step back and think about this statement, it sounds bizarre. Why is it so hard to allow our true selves to exist?

I have worked with many people who dealt with their feelings in relationships by drinking or using. Other people who didn't have substance abuse issues struggled too. It was as if the idea to be your authentic self and speak your truth was never an option because of fear developed from an unsafe childhood. Most folks had spent years learning backward ways to meet their needs.

Co-crazy is repeating a maladaptive behavior such as playing a victim, using anger or manipulation, acting out in some way, making someone feel guilty, or blaming others so you can get what you want. It isn't something that will help you connect with yourself or create true intimacy with others. It will create distance to your true self because you are always in reaction to another, rather than just expressing what you want and need directly.

You may be feeling responsible for your thirty-year-old daughter who just can't seem to get her life together. You keep trying to help her, but she seems to spend a lot of time smoking pot. Her problems become yours as you look up jobs, send her money, and pay for her car to be repaired. You are emotionally tortured about her life even though she feels fine. You may be married to an alcoholic or addict whom you want to change. You may be an alcoholic or addict who has gotten sober, but your life continues to unravel. You may be in a relationship where you know you are controlling, or angry, or terrified of being left, but it's too scary to face alternatives.

I remember one client talking about the upcoming Christmas. She was upset because she had to take her two young children to three different houses on Christmas Day.

I said, "What would make it easier for you? It's tough to travel when you have little ones. Wouldn't it be easier if someone came to your house?"

She said, "Sarah, you know I can't do that."

"Remind me," I said.

"Well, my mother always has to have Christmas dinner at her house at twelve o'clock sharp, but first we have to go to my husband's parents' house for breakfast and have the kids open presents there. Then after lunch, we have to go to Dad's new wife's house and have dessert. We can't have Christmas at our own house until the next day."

Wow. I am not minimizing this gal's pain. It was torture for her and her two small children. They couldn't have Christmas at their own house on Christmas morning—all because she could not tolerate her feelings required to make a change. She couldn't be with her feelings about her *mother* having feelings. She did not have the freedom to make the best choices for her kids and her family. She was still making decisions out of fear. This is a perfect example of how our childhood coping skills are still

CO-CRAZY REMINDER

Dismissing our own needs, feelings, and thoughts leads us to behaviors that we use to numb out the pain of not being seen. Your needs, ideas, and emotions are all essential. Don't dismiss yourself because it will lead to others doing the same. It will also lead to the accumulation of repressed anger, grief, and fear that eventually will come out against yourself or others.

operating. "I have to please Mom, or she will be mad." She is not seven years old; she is thirty-five.

I'm sure there was a long history of Mom being controlling. She didn't want to feel her mother's disappointment or address the changes needed to take place in the relationship. She may have thought her mom wouldn't love her anymore. She may have grown up with active addiction in the household. There are a lot of reasons why this could be happening. She was a prisoner of her past without even knowing it. She did not see the possibility of deciding for herself what she would like to do at Christmas. She was locked in fear, directing her behavior, all based on a child's experience of her mom getting upset.

Take a minute to think about how many of our behaviors are due to the fear of other people having feelings. We tell ourselves the story that we are responsible for others' opinions, rather than doing what is right for us. You can be controlled by a parent, a child, a boss, a partner, a sibling, anyone. All of our early belief systems and coping behaviors are still alive and well and operating at full speed. It's not your job to ameliorate everyone's feelings and make sure they are okay. Let someone be mad at you. Allow people to have their feelings and figure out their own lives. This woman may think this is working but it isn't. The facts are that her kids are stressed and unhappy. She is stressed and unhappy. Her husband is stressed and unhappy. Her belief is that she will make her mother happy. Trust me, her mother is never happy.

Think about every time this woman dismisses her own need to please another—it might happen fifty times a week—from small things to big things. It creates a disconnect inside, a little hole, an inner angst, that over time accumulates and can develop into anxiety, rage, depression, fatigue, detachment from self, the need to escape, chronic exhaustion, busyness, and on and on it goes. It may seem small, but it is not. It is a gradual giving away and dismissing of self, and it creates the need to fill these tiny holes with something else or someone else.

The mother's happiness is not in this woman's hands, but she believes it is. Let Mom have her feelings of disappointment on Christmas. Human beings have feelings; that's what we do. Let people have the dignity of getting to know themselves. Let people learn how to take care of their own business so that they can feel good about it. I know you want to argue with me right now, or give me some examples of how you have helped so-and-so. Go ahead. If your people-pleasing is working, that's great. If it's not, there may be another option. Life is much easier when you don't need to take responsibility for everyone else and can allow people to live their lives. Most importantly, you stay connected to yourself and from there can develop a loving relationship with this remarkable person and create healthier and more satisfying relationships.

Another example is a woman I met while she was tutoring my son in statistics. After one of his sessions, she began to open up to me about her life falling apart due to her son's addiction. She had heard that I worked with addiction and proceeded to ask me a few questions. That very same day she had taken her son to the hospital because he had ingested a bunch of pills prescribed for his attention deficit disorder. These co-crazy stories are about beautiful people. Caring, loving, and kind people. The trouble is what they are doing feels like it's the right solution, but it actually does the opposite of what we want.

The tutor was focused on her son changing, not herself. He was living with her, having returned home for the summer from sophomore year at college. For several months, she would ask me for help. I had given her psychiatrists' names, recommendations for therapists, a list of Al-Anon meetings, books, and articles on codependency and addiction, and even a list of medications that might help.

So why does her life continue to worsen? Her son is still acting out, abusive to her, and continues to get worse. Of course, I'm not blaming her for her son's addiction, but nothing has changed in her life. She has been given tools by me but believes that it isn't about her—it is about her son.

Again, the big lie.

Yes, her son has a drug problem, but he doesn't want to change. Terrified to change herself, she has continued to try to "get him to listen" or "go to a therapist." The suggestions I had given to her were for her, not her son. She remained focused on her son, rather than change herself. *She* didn't go to a therapist, see a psychiatrist, go to recovery meetings, or take better care of herself. She was trying to get someone to change who didn't *want* to change. The addiction was not her responsibility but her *response* to it was.

Her denial is killing her, just like her son's denial is killing him. The difference is that she has the power to change, which will ultimately help her son. This boy is very sick and highly manipulative, but parents react to their children's emotions rather than looking at the facts of the situation. Addicts are brilliant at manipulation. It isn't easy to speak up but it's necessary to change your life. To say no to an addict, to ask him to leave, to tell him you won't give him money, to see him cry, scream, bang his head against the wall, suffer and be in pain is the worst thing in the world. We think that's the worst part of suffering. The deeper, more painful part is experiencing your own feelings of fear, anger, terror, shame, and guilt while this is happening. What would help is not focusing on saving his life but focusing on saving hers first. She is not an anomaly. This behavior is the norm when you love an addict.

Another example of a client struggling with co-crazy is a man who wanted his son to play baseball in the major league someday. This father had brought his son up to play baseball since the age of four. The father's life revolved around his son's

CO-CRAZY REMINDER

We are not responsible for anyone else's thoughts, feelings, or behaviors. We are *only* responsible for our response to them. Mantra: I am accountable for what's in my hula-hoop. That's it.

games, practices, wins, and losses. His moods were highly correlated with his son's baseball career. The problem came when his son was a junior in high school. The boy knew he wasn't going to be a big leaguer. He saw his limitations and didn't want to play anymore. His father was devastated.

The realization for the father was that the drive for his son's success was never about his son. He had wanted to be in the major leagues, but he had suffered a knee injury in college. He also became an alcoholic along the way and was trying to make up for the lost time by controlling his son's sports career. He also was avoiding the problems in his marriage. He started seeing that he needed to grieve the loss of his career, transform his relationship with his son, and face the conflicts in his marriage. His co-crazy was relentlessly projecting his own needs on to his son while avoiding the other issues in his life.

Two important things need to be said. The first is that recovery from addiction and recovery from co-crazy can be difficult and challenging. It can also be exhilarating. I experienced them both as devastating and enlightening, like I had a brain and a heart transplant. After putting down drugs and alcohol, I am a completely different person today, but I'm also the same. My true nature, my spirit, my soul, can be more present now without all the disguises, protections, and escapes.

Co-crazy can be more challenging to identify. When I'm chugging six-packs of beer and snorting lines of coke off the back of a toilet, I have a clue that I have a problem. My co-crazy was harder to see because it is easy to blame and focus on others when their behavior is outrageous. It's much harder to see my part instead of being a victim. I had to transform the way I thought about love and create a new way to be in relationships.

We all develop survival skills while growing up. Say, for example, we have an angry dad, so we learn to stay quiet, not rock the boat, and keep our feelings to ourselves. Some survival skills end up serving us while others are limiting. I felt like nothing was good enough for my own father, so I became an overachiever, trying to get his love. This helped me to get a doctorate degree but does not help when I tie my self-worth to accomplishments to feel loved.

Typical co-crazy character traits are obsessive caretaking and using other controlling behaviors to create a particular outcome with another. Typical co-crazy beliefs, like not feeling wanted or loved, kept getting me into relationships that didn't work. Old practices and old thought patterns still drove my actions in the present. I kept repeating the same dynamics. I chose emotionally unavailable people "to get them to love me." I interpreted these empty victories to feeling lovable, which was more about trying to fill the tiny holes left by my alcoholic mother than anything to do with my partners.

Along the way I did get better at being in relationships. I couldn't have planned my divorce with my first husband, Shane. I couldn't have imagined the relapse of my second husband, Rob, and that our marriage would end. Our marriage was the best relationship I had been in until both our behaviors reached a crisis point: my co-crazy and his addiction.

I think back to being in a session with my mentor, Dr. Berger, at the psychiatric hospital where I did my early training. I was observing a session with a couple, and the husband was a famous writer who had no interest in getting sober. He thought he just needed to "cut down" and he would be fine. What was so noticeable was that the spouse was way more troubled, upset, anxious, despairing, angry, and obsessed with his treatment than the patient.

Every time Dr. Berger tried to discuss her husband's addiction and confront his denial, she would jump in with a bunch of rationalizations and excuses for his behavior. Their marriage was okay; he just needed to stop drinking. At one point in the session, my mentor got so frustrated that he said, "You know you're killing him." I was horrified. I thought, *What does he mean, she is killing him? It isn't her fault. He is the one drinking.*

Twenty-five years later, I know what he meant. When we come face-to-face with the hard truth, they were both killing themselves. So the second thing to be said is that no matter if you are an addict or co-crazy, be kind, gentle, and tender with yourself, and remember that you have a warrior inside of you. Begin the journey to liberation and freedom by staying in your lane, hula-hoop, or whatever image helps you to stay focused on yourself.

Begin to notice how you feel after you take a small step. When I started speaking up for what I needed or set a boundary, I felt a surge of energy. It is as if my true self was returning to my body. I know that sounds nuts, but each small step we take helps us to get ourselves back. We are getting back that precious person we have been giving away to others forever.

LIES

This is a list of some of the lies we tell ourselves when we are in the midst of co-crazy. Pick out a couple of them and begin to notice the lies you tell yourself about your relationship. Now write down the opposite on a 3 x 5 card. Yes, I am suggesting writing affirmations. Train yourself to have new beliefs. We have to start somewhere. Right now, you may believe that critical voice is right. You may even believe some of these are true. Please believe me—they are not.

Examples of Co-Crazy Lies:

- If I just fix this other person in my life, I will be fine.

- If only I could figure out the magic solution I keep missing to solve their problem, then our lives would be perfect.

- My unhappiness is their fault, so why do they keep doing this to me?

- If they would just stop drinking (or anything else that is causing you pain), then I could start my life.

- I'm not good enough, pretty enough, smart enough, talented enough, come from the right family, have enough status, right body, right WHATEVER for them to love me the way I want.

- If I lost weight, they would love me.

- Something is wrong with me.

You get the idea. It isn't about you and it's all about you. Your head is probably spinning. Other people's choices, behaviors, feelings, etc. are not a reflection of you. Your choices, behaviors, thoughts, and feelings are all yours. Remember: "I am not responsible for other people's thoughts, feelings, or behaviors." Period. Give it a try.

* * *

You are me, and I am you. I have struggled for years to find my self-esteem through relationships, and it doesn't work. If you are presently drowning your pain in a substance, it won't help either. If you are currently pre-occupied with someone else's pain so you can feel better and distract yourself from your life, it won't work. My moment of truth came when I couldn't be in denial anymore, and the pain was too great. Human beings are amazing. We can tolerate a great deal of discomfort and pain until we are ready to do something to change. Right?

I know many wonderful people in unhappy relationships right now. Some are addicts, some are married to addicts, some are married to control freaks, some are married to people they can control, but every person resents themselves or someone else. They want someone to change, yet their partners will not change unless they believe there will be a consequence. Who needs to change in this scenario to be happy? The wonderful people. There may be a million reasons why they think they can't change their situation, but it is usually about fear. We have a deep-rooted fear of change, fear of feeling our feelings, fear of hurting someone, fear of disrupting our children's lives, fear of financial ruin, fear of being alone, fear of the unknown, and hundreds of possible concerns operating consciously or unconsciously.

What is empowering is to own it. Just own it. Take responsibility for where you are and what your part is. Whether it is about a partner, a child, or a friend, just take a look at what behavior you continue to do that may be part of the problem— just a thought. Just take a peek. Remember, no blame, no shame, just facts. Here are mine....

2

The Light
Comes On

As I pulled out a pair of shoes from the top of my closet, a handful of loose pills rained down from the shelf. I fell to my knees as I realized my husband had been relapsing for years. Everything began to make sense to me. Memories of our life together flashed before me like the kid's game where you flick cards one by one as the pictures of the story rapidly unfold. At that moment, I had crossed the line between my client's stories and my own. I was the one feeling the urgency and pain of being in crisis.

The truth slammed through me that day in the oval shape of blue-and-white pills tumbling on my head. The scene crashed against my denial like a storm wave pounding against a concrete wall. Somehow, the wall started crumbling and reality came barreling forward into my conscious awareness. The truth, the hard facts of my situation, led to this painful, difficult, stomach-turning, mind-twisting moment where I felt like I was in an alternate universe––while at the same time, in slow motion, I came out of this dream state to wakefulness. I was unable to deny the facts any longer. It was liberating and terrifying.

I had married an addict and alcoholic who had now relapsed, and for two years I tried to make sense of the insanity as I spiraled downward. Attempting this mind trick is a colossal waste of time because there is no way to make sense of madness. I had hyper-vigilantly tried to get proof of the relapse. As if that would have given me permission to take action. I didn't realize I could've taken action any time because his behaviors were already intolerable.

What was wrong with me? I had this pattern of choosing men who I wanted to fix, save, and change while simultaneously thinking they were brilliant, interesting, loving, kind, spiritual people. I should have known by now. After working on myself for years, this pattern seemed relentless. Why was it hard to recognize the repetition of this relational dynamic? It wasn't like I hadn't changed. I had changed a great deal. This ongoing blindness to the truth was insidious, tricky, deep, and subtle. Nobody can control someone else's behavior, but I believed I could.

My focus was always on the other person "who had the problem," but I was the one who felt crazy and confused all the time. I had a relentless preoccupation with my partners' lives. I saw a pattern of years of connections where I got my value and self-esteem from how someone responded to me. I spent decades compromising myself to feel loved. I always wanted to change, heal, and "fix" my intimate partner, family, friends, and colleagues to ease my chronic anxiety. Co-crazy.

This paradigm is a problem. First, the expectation that I could somehow control someone else's feelings, thoughts, or behaviors is a delusion. It is also not my business to try to change someone else. I can support, encourage, or influence, but only when someone wants help, not to satisfy my own agenda. Second, I had completely lost touch with my emotional world and sense of my own identity.

In this dynamic, there are psychological and emotional issues for both people. We want to point the finger and say, "They are the ones with the problem." One person may be more obviously impaired because their problems are more visible, but both suffer. Both people are angry, fearful, and unhappy. They both believe, "If s/he just would . . . then everything would be fine." Believe it or not, both people have similar issues; they just manifest differently. One might be acting out with addiction or overspending or gambling. Still another one is acting out their need for control by over-functioning, using anger or another coping skill learned growing up.

It is often the case in relationships with addiction. My marriage did not start out this way. My husband's behavior had been changing over time, and I kept rationalizing, which allowed me to tolerate my fears. This slow burn of change created a lingering doubt in my reality, which precipitated the slow corrosion of my self-esteem. I had relapsed into my co-crazy behaviors, jumping on the treadmill of insanity as I tried to control something I could not. My progression into darkness and despair was the same as the progression of his addiction.

Trying to communicate with someone in active addiction or some other untruth of dysfunction perpetuates the feelings of craziness. The bizarre style of communication becomes a series of questions, doubt, blame, anger, and self-criticism, where both people are trying endlessly to figure out the other while hiding their own truth. Again, co-crazy.

The addict's world becomes all about defending themselves. They endlessly explain, minimize, and rationalize. Anger outbursts happen when each person blames the other for not trusting them. Everything gets turned around, re-interpreted, thrown at each other like thin spikes slicing bits and pieces of the other person's confidence away. Both partners become crippled by guilt and doubt, and they lose touch with what is real. The addicts can't keep their lies straight, and they don't know where reality ends and fantasy begins. Neither does their partner.

The person trying to control the addict sees their world become smaller and smaller due to the continued focus on the other. As fear increases for the addict's health, life, and sanity, the partner's behaviors become worse. Typically, the co-crazy partner spends hours ruminating on how to "get them to understand." This happens regardless of whether the addict wants to be saved, get better, stop using, or just wants us to get off their backs. We live in the delusion that someday, somehow, we will figure this out and save them. The cosmic joke. It's never going to happen. Meanwhile, our lives are a mess. This is true in any relationship where we want someone to change, not just in relationships with addiction.

Partners of people with addiction problems don't want to see the real truth. It took me two years to finally take action after surviving one crisis after another due to my husband's addiction. All of our troubled situations were neatly explained by the addict as reasonable, somehow making it impossible to see the truth. It became challenging because there were *soft facts* and *hard facts*. For example, it may be a fact when I arrive home from work that my husband is asleep on the couch at four in the afternoon. He could have had a tough day on the job, or he could have taken a handful of Percocets. Hard to know.

Soft facts are those behaviors that appear slowly at first and seem to be completely benign. At times they may seem odd, but they're explainable. Was he late for dinner because his boss asked him to work late? Maybe. *Soft facts* are when a series of incidents happen over days, months, or even years. One episode by itself may not seem strange, but patterns of behavior develop. There are always lengthy explanations. They become more and more colorful over time.

Hard facts are supposed to be the truth, but this is complicated. You would think a *hard fact* is when someone is sitting right in front of you who is intoxicated or high. You'd think it might be obvious, but on numerous occasions, I sat with my husband, saying, *Why doesn't he take his sunglasses off? We're inside!* I have had clients smell saturated with alcohol over the years and tell me they aren't drinking. It is just what we addicts do.

It is a full-time job to try to make someone into who we want them to be. It is also impossible and unrealistic. However, we keep trying. It is exhausting for the one attempting to get control over another. We are met with chronic resistance from the receiver, which creates hurt and resentment on both sides. There is also a type of selfishness where one person believes they know what is right for another. The co-crazy person tries to control another to ameliorate our fear and to feel better ourselves. We don't want to see this because we perceive ourselves as the good guys.

This relational dynamic continues to take both people down.

To put so much effort into something that continues to create struggle, drama, and unhappiness in relationships would make one think to stop the behavior. But we are like junkyard dogs with our jaws gripped on to someone's thigh, feeling like it is the only option. The ongoing mantra just below the surface is: "They need to change so I can be happy."

Many clients' faces flashed before me as I thought of the years spent listening to people struggle to focus on themselves and wanting to change another. I saw the tragedy of lost lives and the absurdities of trying to change someone who isn't interested in changing. After years of counseling people and working with folks in programs, the conclusion: If people would: 1) speak up, and 2) set boundaries, I would not have a job. I'm not kidding.

We care so much about our loved ones. Caring is great. However, putting them before our emotional, physical, and spiritual health out of fear of abandonment, being alone, someone crying, or someone getting angry creates a cycle of chronic disappointment and frustration. Our behaviors become an automatic reaction from past hurts, histories, unresolved expectations, grief, regret, and distorted thinking. This leads to a continuous pattern of similar relationships over and over again where we become the victim.

I will say this throughout the book again and again: It is not just about living with an addict. Clients feel beaten down by the behaviors of people they are trying to help. It could be a child, a parent, a friend, their husband who is depressed, their wife who is compulsively shopping, or their brother who keeps borrowing money. Co-crazy is everywhere. People are angry but they cannot see their participation in the problem.

That day on my knees, broken, and sitting on the floor in that closet was the beginning of a new journey. It was a day that I started, once again, putting into action all the things I had been suggesting to clients for years. I had made many healthy changes prior to the marriage, but my life had gotten way off track. How did it get this bad? I understood addiction from numerous perspectives. I was sober. I had a doctorate in psychology. I worked with people in recovery for twenty-five years. I had also been attending twelve-step family groups for two decades.

Beginning in the mid-1980s, I had done every self-help workshop known to man: Erhard Seminars Training (est), Insight Seminars, a Women, Sex & Power Seminar, ropes courses, bioenergetics, somatic therapies, psychoanalytic therapy, and endless twelve-step meetings. I had recovered from numerous addictions: drugs, alcohol, sex, spending, sugar, cigarettes, and at one point, bubble gum. I was operating like a relief-seeking missile all of my life. I was trying to run away from my own thoughts and pain, although unaware. After putting substances down, I doggedly worked on myself, participated in programs, and achieved success in my field. I had cleaned up my life but still struggled with relationships. Sitting on the floor in that closet, I realized I would be getting divorced for the second time. I was forty-nine years old and had an eight-year-old son. I felt crushed by life.

I was sober but running from myself in sobriety using busyness, work, caretaking for my dad and my husband, seeing clients, and parenting. Everything became a way to not be present. The inevitable disaster occurs when too much energy is going out and not enough recovery coming in. My anger, my grief, my past—everything was catching up with me. Nothing was working, and nothing was going to fix this. Not a line of coke. Not a shot of tequila. Not a chocolate cake. Not another gorgeous man. Just me and God.

3

Rob's Story

In 2006, when I married Rob, he had been sober for years. It never occurred to me he would relapse. It sounds insane now but he was well-known and loved by his AA peers. He had a great program, went to church, had a stable job, sponsored people in AA, spoke at conferences, and had three beautiful adult children. Sounds great, right? Dating was a blissful, love-filled fantasy of Red Sox baseball games, weekends away, lazy days on the beach, going to AA meetings together, and trips to Maine.

After we got married, things started to unravel, beginning with Rob experiencing migraines. I could hypothesize forever about why this was happening. The stress of being married, perhaps a somatic response to early trauma, financial pressure, unresolved rage, but the "why" doesn't matter at this point. Whatever the reason, this is when I started to believe it was my job to solve Rob's problems. It activated my co-crazy in this relationship. He said he had developed the migraines years ago and now they had returned. After numerous doctor's visits, he was prescribed opiates and tranquilizers. I saw him suffering, and some days he could not get out of bed. I felt powerless.

The journey with pain meds began, and looking back now it seems obvious what was happening. He seemed to take all the meds in a short amount of time. The addiction that hides in the darkness of all addicts' minds and hearts, patiently waiting to chew up our souls once again. He was in recovery so I assumed that he knew he needed to be extremely careful with medications, but I soon realized I was living in Fantasyland. I also had a young boy at home, twenty-five clients, and a dad in an assisted-living facility an hour away from where I lived. Pain is a problematic issue in recovery. I don't believe people should suffer, but you have to be *very* careful when pain meds arrive on the scene.

The next thing I knew, I couldn't tell if he was in bed for days because of the migraines or the meds. He seemed completely out of it. The attempts to find a migraine specialist resulted in limited options, and our life together began to break down due to his emotional/physical decline and my response to it. He had started a new business the year before, and it had been highly successful. The company grew, and Rob decided to borrow more money, which created an increase in stress.

Things weren't adding up. I got half-truths of what was going on, but nothing was making sense. His complaints were about his business partner, and how it was his fault that they were in over their heads. The addict blaming others for their problems. More and more medical issues revealed themselves, and Rob was either terrified or med-seeking—probably both. Meds became a way to manage pain and cope with life, and I had a front-row seat to the textbook progression of addiction.

The journey to hospitals and numerous surgeries, doctors, and meds began. He had knee surgery. Then his gallbladder needed to be removed. I could not figure out the truth anymore. Before we met, Rob once told me he had unnecessary back surgery to get drugs. Rob's doctor told me that he *did* need knee surgery, and his gallbladder doctor said it was "the worst gallbladder he has ever seen." Really?

Rob seemed to be in constant pain. Then he was prescribed benzodiazepines because his doctor thought his heart would be impacted due to stress. Rob had heart surgery in his fifties and also had a pacemaker put in. His doctor was worried about his heart. I was concerned about the impending explosion of our lives. Over time, he became irritable, agitated, angry, quiet, withdrawn, and isolated. This was not my husband. He stopped going to meetings and lost most of his friends.

I felt crazy. I knew better. I have a doctorate in psychology. I work with addicts. What was I doing? It was the progression of my co-crazy. Was he seriously using? I felt lost and confused and as if I was living in a different world from my own husband. I would visit my dad in assisted living and feel angry that he was out of control and declining rapidly. I would be mad at my brothers because I felt I was being dumped on. I was angry with clients who weren't getting clean. I really was mad at myself for getting into this mess. I felt like a bad mother. I felt like a victim. I felt helpless, powerless, angry, anxious, and terrified. How could I figure this all out? How could I get him to stop? The delusion of the co-crazy is that the focus becomes an obsession with *their* behavior when the solution was to focus on myself.

Both people in a relapse situation become more and more fearful, angry, anxious, preoccupied, controlling, secretive, and distant. It's natural in these scenarios to want to place blame. What started first? Did Rob begin this journey to insanity with the relapse on drugs, or did I cause it because I became a controlling bitch? Did he relapse because I put too much stress on him? I intellectually knew this was not true, but I felt it deeply.

The truth is nobody causes another person to relapse. Both people are struggling. Both people are in pain. Both people are suffering. Both people are lost and both people need to solve their own problems.

Then two crises happened simultaneously. First, Rob started having chest pains. Five years before this event, he had heart surgery for blocked arteries. One part of his history is that he had an old, deep resentment toward his cardiologist for missing the blockage prior to it being discovered. He got a pacemaker put in but still felt exhausted. He was on a treadmill one day and felt like he was about to collapse. Finally, the surgeon did a catheterization and saw the blockage.

Due to this potentially fatal past error, when Rob began to have chest pain, his anxiety went through the roof. He was in the hospital for a week on heavy doses of pain meds. He kept

complaining that his chest hurt. They did another catheterization. Nothing was found this time, and Rob became enraged.
Most likely this reaction was because he felt shame that he was
proven wrong, caught med-seeking, or angry that the doctor
didn't believe that his level of pain was real. Did I believe Rob
was having chest pain? Yes, I did. Did I believe he thought it was
dangerous? Yes, I did.

I also believe that at some point, Rob just wanted pain meds
and wanted relief from whatever unresolved feelings, hurts,
anger, shame, trauma, or whatever he was trying to avoid. The
drugs stop working as an illusory solution. As an addict's fear of
giving up their substances increases, their moods and behaviors
get worse. It's always easier to look back and see a pattern; it's
much harder when you're in the middle of a crisis.

After his relapse, I became like that cartoon cat that hits the
electrical wire. My body was in a state of feeling overstimulated,
electrified, and exhausted all at the same time. My mind was the
first thing to unravel, and now my body was also collapsing—the
progression of co-crazy at its finest. As the addict gets worse, so
do the people around them. The more out of control it feels, the
more we want control. We begin to experience the same fear,
anger, shame, etc. as the addict, but the behaviors to cope may
be different.

When Rob got prescribed Ativan (a benzodiazepine) for
anxiety after his heart scares, the progression was rapid. He
took a thirty-day supply in five days. I was dealing with someone
who was now under the influence and out of his mind. Worse,
I was also dealing with someone who would experience intense
withdrawal from benzos and opiates when he ran out. I was
terrified of what would happen, but I kept trying to manage
everything. I wanted to be there for my son, let Rob resolve it,
and pretend it wasn't happening. That was when the total shit
show began.

I needed to take action. Maybe not the right action, but
I needed to do something. We went through several conversations about him stopping the pills and that he needed to go to
treatment to get clean again. Then there was the pleading, the

promises, and the "give me one more chance" talks. I told him I would hold the meds and dispense them. It was not a good idea. Suddenly *I* was trying to control his literal intake of substances. This led to his anger coming out at me. He'd say, "But I need another one, I'm in pain."

I was functioning off adrenaline at this point. I had gained a bunch of weight and I couldn't sleep. I was anxious, depressed, and ashamed. I dreamed of escaping. Underneath it all, I was utterly enraged with him and terrified of losing everything. I felt devastated, guilty, and lost. I no longer knew what reality was. I no longer knew the truth. I was depleted and felt absolutely crazy.

The second significant event was that Rob was in a motorcycle accident. You may be thinking, *A motorcycle?* Why would he have a motorcycle when he was using? Exactly. When he was recovering from his knee surgery, he said, "Sarah, I've always wanted a motorcycle. My kids are grown, what do you think?" I've always loved motorcycles. Images of us riding up the beautiful coast of Maine flashed in my brain. I thought he deserved to be happy. He said he was a conscientious and responsible rider.

One Sunday he went for a ride and arrived back at the house all battered and not making sense. He had been "driving slowly on a back road when a woman pulled in front of him." He had a shattered shoulder, a fractured scapula, broken ribs, cracked collarbone, and bruises everywhere. I found all this out later when the ambulance I called rushed him to the hospital. How the f**k did he ride home? Shock? High doses of meds? Who knows?

I will never know the complete truth of what happened that day, but I can be sure it was the result of substance abuse. Usually, when the craziness of addiction hits your relationship, strange things start to happen, but there is always more to the story. Unfortunately, this led Rob to a three-month stint on the couch, taking lots of meds for his injuries. Everything was disintegrating. Over time, I would say, "You need to change" or "I can't do this." I would then immediately say to myself, "Sarah, he was in an accident. Come on, be nice."

This was the co-crazy flip-flop between wanting to kill the

addict and then feeling sorry for them. What was coming out of his mouth was everything I wanted to hear. "I'll go back to meetings, I'll get into therapy, I'll get off the meds, I'll call some friends in AA, I'll get a job." His company had gone bankrupt by this time. What made things murkier was that maybe some of these things were half-ass really happening, so there was a delusion that maybe he was "trying." All bullshit.

Over time, it became more apparent that he was in active addiction. I somehow broke through my fog and looked at the facts of what was happening. The new job was suddenly gone for some reason other than it being his fault. The friends in AA "had changed," and not surprisingly, everyone else was the problem. Every excuse and rationalization became Rob's reality. At the same time, I was feeling beaten down, checked out, and paralyzed. I was struggling to get through the day. I was trying to be a good mom and support my son, get more in control of an out-of-control situation, take more responsibility, and manage more. I told myself, "I've got this."

It's sad to say, but toward the end, the person I loved became someone I couldn't stand to look at. I began to avoid him and realized I couldn't do it anymore. The day I found the pills was a relief. I confronted Rob, and like a scared little boy, he sobbed and begged me not to ask him to leave. It was one of the hardest things I've ever done, but my anger was a great motivator. Once I got so done, so angry, it was hard to feel compassion anymore.

When I crossed that line into being more angry than loving, it led me to take action I couldn't take previously. But I didn't want to be angry forever. It killed me to make Rob leave because I was an addict too. Anger is a "luxury for normal men," and I had to step out of the crisis and focus on myself and my son. It helped to set the hard boundary—the one I knew I had to set, the one I knew was the only way out even though someone was begging me not to do it. I had to. I hated him. I hated myself. I was trying to save us both. I had to accept that I could not solve his problem. I surrendered to my powerlessness over his addiction.

How many times did I have to hit another emotional bottom in my recovery program? After finding the pills in that closet, I crawled back to my recovery program and collapsed into the loving arms of my fellow travelers. I saw that the minute I began to worry more about my husband than myself, I lost the connection to me. I had begun to slack on attending meetings and had become isolated. I did not see my own mental and physical health deteriorating. This was the insanity of the progression of both the addict and his co-crazy partner—me.

I was having trouble sleeping. I was diagnosed with depression. I felt anxious all the time. I had no energy. My body ached endlessly. I was constantly irritable, agitated, and angry. I was preoccupied with my fear of the future and overwhelmed by the thought of change. I felt chronically guilty. I did not know who I was anymore. Mainly, I thought, *How the f**k did I get myself into this?*

As our partners' addiction or other behavior progresses, our co-crazy thoughts, feelings, and behaviors increase and amplify. As fear and anger progress, the need to control grows. As the need to monitor something I can't control progresses, depression, anxiety, and shame also progress.

Thinking becomes obsessive and delusional, while numerous cognitive distortions such as rationalization and minimization will dominate perceptions of situations brought about by the addict. The body starts to break down, and feelings swing to extremes from repression to acting out. Behaviors are all just adaptations to survive. The classic move is to put your head down and power through. Eventually, the crash will come.

This is what happens in co-crazy, but because we are focused on the other and detached from ourselves, we don't even realize we are decompensating. Eventually we will be a broken, empty shell. We will not know how we feel, we will not know what we think, and we will not know what we need. We have lost ourselves due to our obsession. Both people have gotten worse, but the delusion is that we believe we are saving someone else. That is unvarnished co-crazy.

At the time of Rob's relapse, I was in so much pain I was

willing to try anything. The irony was that I had a previous crash ten years before when I left my first marriage. I thought, *Crap, haven't I resolved this stuff yet? Come on.* I had changed but ended up in a similar situation. Why was this happening?

My growth over the years in sobriety had been mainly progressive, with some twists, turns, and setbacks. Recovering addicts and alcoholics keep coming back to our recovery tools, with each new set of circumstances being an opportunity for growth and acceptance of life on life's terms. Getting to know myself again and again at a deeper level is a continuous joy and endless torture. Ha. Was this my own life lesson to resolve? Was this some kind of karma?

I discovered that my life was still being run to a significant degree by my past. There were many belief systems I created, many feelings I repressed, and many behaviors I adapted, which developed a personality more and more distant from my true self. I was born an extraordinary being, a child of God. Due to ongoing situations and relational dynamics, I learned behaviors that allowed me to survive within those environments, but they were no longer working. So now what?

The Other F Word: *Feelings*

In households where nobody is speaking about their feelings or acknowledging feelings of others, or expressing feelings appropriately, you will likely end up with a conflicted relationship to even *having* feelings. Either you will be afraid of having feelings, you will repress them, or you'll tell yourself you shouldn't have them. You might get anxious when you start to notice a feeling and then experience fear about someone getting angry if you express it. The tragedy is that we decide we shouldn't feel even though it is just what our systems do. Unfortunately, many of us learned that we needed to hide them, dismiss them, avoid them, or not show them in order to survive in our dysfunctional environment.

Not having space to identify, experience, and express one's feeling-states leads to a multitude of co-crazy behaviors. Not having people validate and empathize with your feelings leads to always guessing what is happening inside and out. It becomes an endlessly confusing task to identify our internal experience with nobody available to confirm our reality. We feel wrong for having feelings. We begin to experience a low level of anxiety out in the world and an inability to trust.

If you grow up in a home where you say, "You seem angry" and the person yells, "I'm not angry," you begin to distrust your perceptions. Whatever you grew up with becomes the norm. We don't realize our norms may be different from other people's. Moreover, maybe our norms of not expressing our feelings have served us well in specific environments. Our personalities become all or nothing, rather than experiencing a variety of feeling states.

If thinking is distorted, and we are repressing or avoiding feelings, we are probably acting out with our behaviors. As a young child, I learned to please others to get my value.

Some of my adaptive behaviors were:

- Avoiding negative feelings.
- Keeping a false front of happiness all the time.
- Never getting upset.
- Repressing, pretending, denying my negative thoughts and feelings.
- Focusing on achieving.
- Acting out to feel better with food and later with sex and then substances.
- Avoiding saying what I thought or felt.

The ongoing trouble with this way of existing was that I moved further away from what was truly happening inside me. My behaviors were motivated by a depletion, a need to get something, or a fear of never being enough. The more painful it got on the inside, the riskier the behaviors became to move away from the pain. When the obsession with food stopped working, I moved to alcohol, drugs, and then to boys. I needed more ways of moving away from myself as the internal states intensified.

The co-crazy development works to escape through whatever I can to remove the focus from my pain and try to fix something outside of myself. It initially feels like a solution to check out, but inevitably it adds to the list of regrets and shame that will have to be faced eventually. What begins as a source of relief to survive a stressful childhood then develops into a need to continue to cope by sacrificing yourself through addiction or co-crazy behaviors. In the end, it all stops working and becomes the source of your deepest pain.

The bottom line of co-crazy recovery is becoming familiar with what is happening inside of you so you don't need to escape, whether it is addiction or co-crazy. It is just the beginning of the topic of feelings, just so you know. But don't worry. It is a gentle journey and you are never alone.

Leaving Crazy Town

Black Belt Self Care: Having Compassion for Yourself

One of my closest friends told me a story about going to couple's therapy for the first time with her alcoholic husband. The therapist specialized in addiction and spoke with her husband about his potential sobriety as my friend looked on anxiously, wondering, *What can I do!?* Like me, she was stuck in her over-functioning mode of trying to save her husband rather than focusing on herself. She wanted the therapist to give her an action step. The therapist turned to her after a while and said, "What do you need to do? You just need to rest."

By the time a person walks into a therapist's office due to co-crazy behaviors, she or he will be exhausted, anxious, frustrated, angry, and depleted. When I finally asked my husband to move out until he got sober, I hadn't even realized the extent of my utter exhaustion. I was so familiar with pushing through the fatigue that when I finally stopped, I crashed physically and mentally. Just rest. Stop and breathe. The same thing happened when I got sober. I hadn't realized that the drugs were the substance that kept me awake and moving. I discovered feeling tired and depleted was normal. I needed to work on recovery, but I also needed to rest.

Practice buddha-like principles. When you're hungry, eat; when you're thirsty, drink; and when you're tired, rest. So simple, yet it confronts old belief systems about slowing down. For many people, these solidified ways of doing too much are contrary to self-care. Moreover, for many folks, slowing down means we are then stuck with experiencing our thoughts and feelings. It may be challenging if we have been in denial or avoidance states for a long time. This is a big deal.

We all have the potential to be hard on ourselves. If we grew up in insanity or chaos we might have issues with perfectionism, striving, being good enough, self-reliance, and comparing. If we are in a co-crazy relationship with anyone, most likely we are overdoing and suffering. If we are someone recovering from any addiction, we are often beating ourselves up for not doing enough or not having the perfect solution or answer.

It's hard enough just to get through the day sometimes without hearing that critical voice inside. At one point, I remember my sponsor saying, "Do you have any compassion for yourself?" This question landed. I had been striving all my life for success, to be loved, to help others, and to feel okay about myself. Meanwhile, my mental health kept getting worse and worse. I had to take some time and say to myself, *This isn't right, you don't treat others this way. Stop being so mean to yourself!* This voice has evolved over the last thirty years to a more loving one.

I heard a friend of mine speak of her struggle with self-criticism. She told me that now when she talks to herself, she uses gentle, kind words as if she is speaking to a child she loves. She will say, "Come on, sweetie, it is okay, it isn't that bad." I love this idea. I have begun to have more compassion for all I have gone through and be at a new level of peace with my past. No judgment.

Leaving Crazy Town

Finding Your Voice: Speak Up

The most critical aspect of our journey to less co-crazy is learning and practicing to speak up. When we don't speak our truth, we end up repressing our authentic thoughts and feelings. This leads us away from the true connection we want with people. For years, while growing up with four brothers, my alcoholic mom, and a dominating father, it was challenging to feel like I had something worth saying and to find the courage to speak.

Finding someone to listen and validate your reality is critical to beginning to get to know yourself. Many people stop speaking up when they perceive unspoken or spoken messages from their parents that their voice is not important. Start to take the risk of speaking up and sharing your truth. Getting validated puts you on the daring road to freedom and authenticity.

There needs to be a safe environment to begin to speak up. If you are not living in a situation where you are being heard, find a therapist or people who will listen. Believe that you have something to say, and that there is a way through. Find people who will respect you and give you space and time to be understood. We can also practice speaking up anywhere and with anyone. It can be when you're buying shoes, and you don't want the pair the woman has shown you. I once bought a pair of shoes because I didn't want to hurt the saleswoman's feelings. I'll admit to being co-crazy—I felt guilty to tell her I didn't need them. I didn't have the power to ruin her day.

This can be the beginning of saying your truth because it is not a 911. Practice with relationships that are less activating rather than dealing with someone you are deeply attached to. Nobody in this situation is going to die over the decision to not purchase a pair of shoes, although it may feel that way inside. Speaking up in deeper relationships can be more challenging, unless you're pissed off all the time and yelling, but ultimately that doesn't work for anyone. If you want to feel freedom, feel lighter, and feel less anxiety and depression, begin to share what

CO-CRAZY REMINDER

There is a saying, "We are as sick as our secrets." Secrets make us sick.

you genuinely think and feel. It will change the way you stand in yourself.

When we stop being preoccupied with how the world responds to us and start to focus on what is going on inside of us, we will begin to build a more robust sense of self. If we can honor ourselves first and communicate our thoughts and feelings without shame, it will increase our self-esteem. Have you ever revealed a secret or told someone something you did that you felt terrible about? It's as if your body does a huge sigh of relief. It feels as if energy has been released and your body can settle more.

If we begin to share who we are, we can let go of previous behaviors we used to hide our feelings from ourselves. What we thought were character traits, such as compulsively talking or not talking or isolating or being extroverted, may partly be due to the need to distance ourselves from the internalizations of the past, and we become all the subsequent skills developed to cope.

Sometimes when we are getting our voices back, we begin to blurt things out. It may not be the best option but it is better than repression and fear. One client impulsively quit her job because she hated it but hadn't thought about how she was going to pay her rent. So don't be unconscious as you begin to get your voice back. There is a balance between beginning to express who we are and telling our husbands we had an affair for ten years. Bringing honesty back into a relationship takes time and humility. Get some support and don't slam other people with the truth if you can help it.

It is uncomfortable, it may be new for you, and it may change relationships, but having integrity with a partner can only bring deeper intimacy, even if it is hurtful. It is the beginning of believing that we care about ourselves more than accommodating another's feelings. If you want to feel freedom, peace, serenity, and self-esteem, then find your voice and take risks with people. It requires tapping into a long covered-up inner source of courage and trust, but it is the beginning of getting your true self back.

MY STORY: How Did I Catch It? The Progression of Addiction and Co-Crazy

"My favorite drink is a blackout"

—Friend at a twelve-step meeting

4

When the Crazy Began

I didn't pop out of the womb feeling responsible for other people. My earliest memory of my relationship with my mother is from when I was four years old. I was attending pre-school, and one day I was climbing a jungle gym, and I fell and tore up my knee. When my mother picked me up in her green-paneled Chevy wagon, I was nervous climbing into the back seat. I felt ashamed, like it was wrong that I hurt myself. When I was in the back seat of that station wagon, I wasn't worried about my knee or the blood seeping through the bandage. I was concerned about my mother being upset. I remember feeling as though she was mad that I got hurt.

In reality, my mother had four children by then. She was trying to get through the day without killing anyone. When I look back at this scene from her perspective, she probably was upset because she had to find someone to watch my little brother, or couldn't go to her one exercise class a week, or she couldn't finish food shopping for a family of six. Still, in my little brain, I was already preoccupied with her feelings. I remember I tried to stay quiet and not say anything. Why did a four-year-old already feel responsible for her mother's emotions?

My mother was a stay-at-home mom, and at one point had

five children under the age of ten. One of my positive early memories of her was her waking me up one night after she came home drunk from a party. She walked into my bedroom with something underneath her coat. She stood next to my bed and slowly unwrapped her arms and gently handed me a beautiful white kitten with a black spade on its back. I was so happy but also confused. *Why is she doing this for me?* It was one of the first times she expressed a loving, thoughtful gesture, just toward me. It felt good and awkward and scary.

My early years were full of plenty of fun memories with my brothers. We had a pond down the street where we would spend hot afternoons walking around the murky water with our feet squishing through black mud, trying to see the two-feet-long snapping turtle we swore lived beneath the surface. We played kickball in the side yard with the entire neighborhood of twenty children, where we ran around slate bases and screamed as we slid into home plate. Early evening barbecues turned into hours spent bouncing on a pit trampoline my parents had installed after we had attended a summer camp where they were popular. Outside our house, life was full of adventures, picking wild blackberries in the woods across the street or building dirt forts in deep holes in the backyard.

Inside, the house was different. I often refer to my childhood home as The Prison. It was a large red brick house with white trim and a big side yard. From the outside, it looked beautifully maintained with a lush lawn and beautiful gardens. White columns framed the front door. The facade was pristine, but when I stepped inside, all I felt was anxiety because everything was unpredictable. The level of tension depended on how much my mother drank that day *and* what mood my dad was in. I could never know or plan for what was about to happen. All I knew was that the anxiety would start to escalate around four o'clock every afternoon because Dad would be coming home.

My parents' nightly ritual was to argue. By dinnertime, my mother would be halfway to buzz town and begin to slur her words while she attempted to light her cigarette. We braced ourselves for the eventual eruption when we all noticed that she was lighting her cigarette backward and her words weren't making sense. Suddenly, we would realize simultaneously that Dad knew she had been drinking. Then the silence that lasted forever. Some nights, the fight would begin right there at the dinner table. They would scream at each other and Dad would leave the table in disgust. Most of the time, my brothers and I learned to eat as fast as possible so we could quickly avoid the potential scene of conflict. "May I please be excused?" and the accompanying thought, *Please, dear God, let me be excused.*

It was not only about my mother's drinking. My father had an anger problem. He had served in the military in World War II and had undiagnosed PTSD. He was a mixture of self-centeredness, narcissism, and a wounded child. He could also be brilliant, entertaining, and the life of the party. I was scared of my father for years because it wouldn't take much for him to get irritated, which led me to wanting to be perfect and not disappoint him.

He loved the French language. I took four years of French but barely made it to the second-year workbook. It was a source of great frustration for my father. Sitting at his desk at night and reviewing French vocabulary words with him was like stabbing myself with pencils. I was fearful of making a mistake. I dreaded his sighs of disappointment, eventually leading to his anger and gestures of resignation. I knew this was important to him, but I could not get it.

My underlying obsession with how to make things okay for my parents began in those early years. Their feelings became my priority. The saner they were, the safer I felt. If I could make them happy, then I could get some peace. My body was in a constant state of tension, and I began having chronic stomachaches, which ironically led to a food obsession to soothe myself. I developed an eating disorder as a pre-teen and became obsessed with the sweet taste of sugar. I couldn't get enough. It was something I could count on to give me relief from the anxiety and to make my stomach feel better temporarily.

The craving for sugar began in elementary school. My brothers and I went home for lunch every day from school. When returning to school, we would stop at Wards Drug Store, where they had an enormous penny candy selection. At the store, my siblings and I were given a little paper bag to fill up with a variety of Tootsie Rolls, Mary Janes, Cherry Stix, caramel Bulls-Eyes, and Smarties. After loading up at lunchtime, I'd hide my bag in my desk, and when the teacher wasn't looking, I would sneak my hands inside to grab a treat.

As an adolescent, my friends and I went to the ice-cream store every afternoon after school. It was fun to ride our bikes to the town square and get a booth at Brigham's and feel like adults for a while. I loved lime rickeys. I'm not sure what was in them, but they tasted like a fancy adult drink. Then the Brigham's vanilla with sprinkles, which is now famous in supermarkets around the world. *Oh, the delight, the sweetness, and the relief.* I didn't know at that point what was happening to me. I just knew I didn't want to feel and wanted to escape because I felt trapped.

When I was an older adolescent, I remember begging my father to divorce my mother and ranting to my mother to divorce my father. I felt like it wasn't fair for us kids to suffer the consequences of their drama. The ongoing joke in my family was that my parents had a fight that lasted forty-two years. The topic didn't matter—they *never* agreed on anything. When asked at her fiftieth high school reunion what her most significant accomplishment was, my mother answered, "Staying married to the same man for forty-two years."

I believe my parents stayed together because they were terrified of change. Maybe it was love in some dysfunctional, bizarre, distorted manifestation and expression. Perhaps they were afraid to be alone. Maybe they were scared of what the unknown might bring. My father said to me once, "If we got divorced, how do I know it will be any better than it is now?" My response: "How could it get any worse?"

When we were in high school, my mother had an affair with her cousin's husband. He was a smart, gentle, outdoorsy guy, and they would meet up during the day. Often, my brothers or I would see them driving in town, or when we came home from school he would be leaning against the kitchen counter with a beer in his hand. It was so crazy that this affair was going on right under my dad's nose. One day, I was so angry about harboring this secret that I said to my mother, "Either you tell him or I will!" My mother's response was, "Well, just don't tell Sam's wife; she has threatened suicide." Oh great. Now I'm suddenly responsible for whether her lover's wife lives or dies.

I had been mad at my mom for years. I was the only girl, and I never felt like she liked me. I was angry with their insanity, I was mad that I had to hold secrets, I was angry that they were so f**ked up, I was mad that I didn't feel like I had a mother, and I was angry that I had felt responsible for my dad for years. At that moment, I decided I'd had enough. I thought, *No more. It is not my problem.*

So one night, my dad returned home from work, and I asked to talk to him. We were sitting upstairs in his bedroom where he'd sit at his desk and watch TV most evenings. I said, "Dad, Mom is having an affair with Sam Wilson." I didn't know how to say it, so I just spit it out. I looked up at my dad sheepishly, and he paused and leaned back in his desk chair, smoking a cigar. He said, "Sarah, your mother and I have a lot of problems, but Sam Wilson isn't one of them."

I was shocked. I had worried about my father finding out for years. My brothers and I often spoke about it. I was so tired of feeling responsible for my parents' feelings. For years, I carried the shame and guilt about covering up my mom's behavior and fear about what my dad would do if he found out. As I discovered . . . not a thing.

I'm not sure if my dad was in some form of denial and didn't believe me. Or that for some reason, he somehow did not see this guy as a threat. I mean, Sam Wilson was spending afternoons with my mother in the Holiday Inn! Why was I trying to change people who didn't even see that there was a problem?

I told my dad because I couldn't take it anymore.

The older I got, the worse my parents' problems became, and the fights escalated. My brothers and I were tired of it. We began to intervene and yell back. This was the set-up for my future thinking patterns beginning with the preoccupations: How could I stop my mother from drinking? How could I stop my dad from being so miserable and pissed off? I tried to be a good girl to make people happy. Bake those cookies, do those dishes, sit next to Dad at the dinner table, don't speak up, don't get upset, do what your father tells you, pretend everything is fine, and for God's sake, don't tell anyone how you feel.

My parents did stay together until my mother passed away. My mother died of cancer, which I'm sure was complicated by years of alcoholism, two packs of Marlboros a day, and eating steak and cottage cheese for breakfast. My father lived to be ninety-two, at times still ruminating, "What could I have done better to stop your mother's drinking?"

That is a tragedy. It's both tragic that my mother died living with active alcoholism, and that my father died still thinking he could have changed it. Co-crazy.

The relentless preoccupation with the job of fixing my parents was the beginning of my delusional thinking. It was not going to happen. But I believed that if I could somehow get them to stop fighting and find some peace in our house, maybe I could feel safe. Then, maybe my mother would tell me I'm beautiful, or maybe my father would leave me alone. The symbiotic relationship between the family situation and the distorted belief systems were solidified. I now got my value from what I could do for others, not from my sense of self. Later, alcohol and drugs were the roads to Numbland. Not the best idea.

5

My Attempts
at Escape

The first day I drank, I was sixteen, and I got obliterated. I can taste it even now when I think about it forty-five years later. I decided I was going to have a beer with some girlfriends and asked one of my brothers to buy it. As a joke, he bought something nicknamed The Green Death—and the next day, I knew why. I was sick for days. Even though I got sick, I was excited to do it again. It eased all my tension, anxiety, anger, feelings of inferiority, and my shame about my body. When I drank, I could make people laugh. When I drank, I didn't have to feel alone and different. When I drank, I didn't have to feel the pain of being the first girl dropped off on a Friday night from a carload of teenage couples.

I was a junior in high school and forty pounds overweight. Being overweight as a teenage girl filled me with shame and embarrassment. It's as if everyone could see how f**ked up I was because of how I looked. *If they only knew.* My total lack of self-confidence was exacerbated by the fact that my four brothers were lean, tall, and athletic with lots of gorgeous friends. It ended up being a lethal combination of intense self-loathing, deep longing, and a vast fantasy life. I had crushes on many boys who saw me as so-and-so's sister. Sixteen was the age when the ache for some boy to like you, to look at you in that special way, just to see you, and pay attention to you, want you, was so deep that it took my breath away.

I was starting down a long road of looking for someone to fill that emptiness. I would think to myself, *Maybe this person will make me feel whole.* It transitioned from an obsession with my parents, to an obsession with food, to booze, to boys, to cocaine. I would unendingly put my self-esteem, love for myself, self-worth, and sanity in the hands of some boy who had no idea he was supposed to be the answer to all my problems. He didn't realize that it was his job to love me so intensely and profoundly that I would finally feel lovable—an impossible task.

When the drinking started in tenth grade, I lived in the delusion that it helped. My memory of drinking in high school is a blur, but I do remember sleeping with my best friend's boyfriend. She wouldn't put out. I was bombed, and so was he, and I'm still not sure why I did it. Maybe to feel wanted, to feel okay, just once. My drunken rationale was I didn't want to be the fat girl that nobody wanted to date. I'm not even sure if we ever spoke again, the boy or my friend.

In the summer between junior and senior year, I went with a group of girls from around the country on a program called Operation Crossroads Africa. It was amazing. Ten girls traveled to an island in the Netherlands Antilles to help build homes and roads and support the island people. I was suddenly not seen as the overweight redhead who didn't fit in. I was now a girl who people wanted to be around. Magically, the island happened to be populated by about seventy-five percent men, so the odds were excellent. They only sold Heineken beer. It was heaven.

I was sixteen years old, and for the first time, I was surrounded by people from different cultures, races, and backgrounds, all coming together for the common good. Within a week, we all had boyfriends, and within ten days, we had all gone to the island doctor and gotten an experimental birth control shot that wasn't legal in the US. I didn't get my period for a year and a half. I started having sex with a twenty-six-year-old man, and I felt loved and wanted. I'd never felt happier. I even thought about living there for the rest of my life. Life was simple, and I longed for simple. All summer, we drank, laughed, hung out with men, danced, swam, and helped the local people. We learned about a completely different way of life. I felt at ease for the first time in my life. I even lost twenty pounds. Life was blissful for me there, and for the first time I had a purpose.

When I returned home, I went into culture shock. My parents had sent me to prep school because I was flunking out of the public high school. So I returned to this new school where I felt out of place and had no friends. I thought all the other girls were beautiful. The longing for the boy's attention did not stop, and I quickly gained back forty pounds. My first addiction was in full force again. My senior year was an empty landscape of unhappiness and loneliness. I got mono and barely made it to graduation.

I remember the day I graduated like it was yesterday because it was so humiliating. We all had to wear long white dresses. I had bought this gauze, ankle-length, white sundress with an elastic neckline that you could pull down over your shoulders. It cinched at the waist, and I got somewhat of a waistline out of it. To wear this dress, you had to wear a slip underneath. I bought a sleeveless slip that seemed to work holding my breasts together. By the age of seventeen, I was a double D.

After the ceremony, all the teachers stood in a line while all the graduates had to pass through this line and shake their hands. By the time I got to my third handshake with the football coach, Mr. Simon, my slip had dropped to my waist, and my double Ds poured out into my gauze top. Good Lord. I'm not sure who noticed this, or maybe who didn't, but my face turned bright red, and I rushed my way through the line bent over with my arms wrapped around me while holding my breasts together. I was mortified.

I was in no shape to go off to college, so I deferred to a small Midwest school with the hope that I would be ready in a year. My father famously said, "Sarah, you just need to sow your wild oats." Probably not the best advice to a budding alcoholic. The year between high school and college, my drinking escalated, and my affair with cocaine began. Things were now increasing from food to booze to boys to drugs—this was the progression of my addiction. I had several jobs that year. I worked at a nursing home where the head nurse was a coke dealer. It was my gap year of addiction management. *Perfect.* I ended up working at numerous bars, restaurants, and diners. I eventually moved to Miami for the winter.

When I lived in Miami for those five months, it was as if my addictions were stuck on the fast forward button. My friend Sharlene and I moved down there to enjoy the weather, make some money, and meet people. I ended up working at a hotel in Key Biscayne, where my family vacationed when I was a child. A wealthy neighbor of ours spent the winters at this same hotel. When I dropped our family friend's name to the manager Mario, I was hired on the spot. Without realizing it, it was a controversial hire. All of the waiters were older Cuban men, and many of them had worked there for years. This was their livelihood. I walked in there as an eighteen-year-old naive, troubled, suburban white girl from Boston looking to have fun. Mario felt obligated to do my neighbor this favor.

During this time, I felt lost and had no conception of my own identity. My addiction was moving fast, which was a bad recipe for a young girl waiting tables in the cocaine capital of the world. I had no sense of self, I was looking for approval every-where, and felt shame about my weight. I was still yearning to feel okay, thinking somehow it would magically come from the next drink, the next line of coke, or the next boy.

I lasted five months in Miami but it felt like years. I would wake up at four o'clock in the morning to take three buses out to Key Biscayne in the dark. I got into lots of trouble with men during this time. Walking the streets at that early hour to take the buses to start my shift at seven seemed to be a fertile ground to meet crazy men. I couldn't feel anything but longing and des-peration for love and escape.

I frequently gave my body away in hopes that someone would fill the emptiness. I was a walking zombie, thoroughly checked out, and felt like I was acting in my own life. I don't remember three days of my life because I popped a bunch of quaaludes and

Seconals. There are vague memories of my downstairs neighbor's husband. In brief moments of awareness, I wondered what was wrong with me.

One night I slept on the screened-in porch and was startled awake in the early morning by a man shouting at me while holding a gun. He said to me, "Are you Jessie Gomez's girlfriend?" I didn't have a boyfriend, but we had hung out with a guy named Jessie and his friend Tony for several weeks doing endless amounts of drugs until they stole our money. The man was a police officer who told me Jesse had shot his partner the previous evening. I was shocked and numb. I couldn't feel anything anymore. What was I doing? We spent the day driving around in his tan Buick looking for Jesse even though I knew *nothing* about him or where he lived.

A couple of weeks later, I stood in line for a couple of hours to get into the prison to see Jesse and find out what happened. When I got to the front of the line, I wasn't on his visitor list. Embarrassed and humiliated in front of one of my two brothers who had come to "rescue me," I walked away, wondering what was real. The sad thing is that what disturbed me the most was thinking that he didn't care about me. This was insanity. Did I really care about what some strange man—probably a sociopath with a long record—thought about me? I knew my mind wasn't right, but I was lost and confused.

My brothers came down to save me from myself but we ended up doing lots of coke and partying for a couple of days instead. Miami in the 70s. The fact is, nobody could save me at this point in my addiction. They were trying to hold onto the tail of a jet about to take off. I eventually returned home to Boston in just enough time to head to Chicago and start college.

6

The Progression

My parents shipped me out a few days early to a college in the Midwest in hopes that I would transform my life. I had three tattoos by now, including on my shoulder and ankle, which would be visible to my new Midwest pals. I began college in 1978, and the only girls who had tattoos were at biker rallies. Moreover, I was attending Lake Forest College after living the life of a drug addict/alcoholic for the previous three years. What could possibly go wrong?

When I arrived in Chicago feeling utterly unprepared, it felt like a redo of my prep school nightmare. I only lasted one semester. My drug addiction progressed and the law was now getting involved. I should have had a jacket with the word Troubled with a capital T printed on my back. Everywhere I went, chaos followed me, but I didn't know I was the common denominator.

I was there alone except for the sports teams. My welcoming party happened in the cafeteria. I went by myself, and the cafeteria was empty except for the football team. They were all living it up at a table, cheering, making loud noises, doing what football teams do. I walked by them in what I thought was a decent looking calf-length peasant skirt and a beautiful white blouse, and my tattoos were showing. I got some food and went and sat at a table. I forgot ketchup and went back up to get some, and when I got back to my seat, my tray and my food had been trashed. It was everywhere.

The irony about this story is that I don't know why this happened to me. Perhaps they thought I was weird, maybe they didn't like me for some reason, or they thought I was cute? Maybe it was the tattoos? What sticks with me is that I made up a story about how boys felt about me. It confirmed the already established beliefs that I was ugly, unwanted, and unlovable. The crazy thing is a month later, my friend gave me a picture of a girl with long hair and a great smile sitting on a couch in our dorm room. I thought she was pretty. I said to this friend of mine, "Who is this girl?" He thought I was kidding. It was me. I had no idea what I looked like and really would never know. I was so alienated from my own experience; I had no idea how the world saw me. Can someone say "detached"?

The fall semester in Chicago turned out to be a complete disaster. There are many things we do that seem to make sense at the time but are utterly insane in hindsight. I came home for Thanksgiving break to see my family. Unfortunately, I was still doing cocaine and owed my coke dealer big dough. I had this brilliant plan of getting him to front me an ounce of cocaine and take it back to college, so I could sell it and pay him the money I owed him. If I weren't a drug addict, this would have been a great idea, but by the time I got off the plane in Chicago, I had snorted a bunch of it. Then, when I got back to the dorm and saw my buddies, the party continued. It was all gone within forty-eight hours.

Take three college kids' minds and add the fact that I now owed three grand to a drug dealer when I got home at Christmas, and we urgently came up with a plan. I convinced my two best friends to help me "rob a bank." We were going to have Cindy from Nashville drive the getaway car. She had an adventuresome spirit, and she was up for it. We would steal blank checks from my roommate just because she didn't party, had money, and I was desperate. We then forged them for the amount needed and drove to her bank, and one of us went into the front entrance. The rest of us went to the drive-through, and we would meet up later, hopefully several thousand dollars richer—the naiveté of youth and the stupidity and selfishness of a drug addict.

We didn't pull it off. My friend came walking out of the bank, all smiles, holding up the cash, but when we went through the drive-through, we must have looked suspicious because the bank teller started questioning us. So what else could we do but take off? We soon found out when returning to the dorm that three of our friends who had similar features to us and were walking in town had been mistakenly taken in for questioning. After they convinced the police they were innocent, the cops told my friends to communicate to the real perpetrators to be at the police station the next morning at nine a.m. sharp.

The next day the three of us went down to the police station and we were booked. My father had my mug shot in a locked box for years, a photo with me in my faded green crew sweater, a look of terror in my eyes, holding up the black number plate in front of my chest. Little did we know that check fraud is a *felony*. Holy shit, that was bad.

Someone was watching out for me because the police and the courts concluded it was a college prank, and the drugs were never mentioned. We all got sent home and kicked out of school for a semester. My friends went back the next year and ended up graduating. Thank God. My journey continued on the path of destruction and numbness until complete. My father told me the police had said that I wasn't allowed back in Chicago.

7

When My Addiction and Co-Crazy Collide

My life became a series of troubled alcoholic relationships, temporary jobs, and weak attempts at education. I was headed to the bottom but not soon enough. In twelve-step programs, we talk about "incomprehensible demoralization." These two words accurately describe the life of an addict or alcoholic. For five years, it just kept getting worse and worse. There were legitimate attempts to get my life back together, whether I started a good job or tried a different school. Still, the disturbing and deadly thing about addiction is that denial permeated every cell in my body, and nothing changed. The insanity continues due to the blindness of drugs and alcohol being the problem.

We always think it's something else, someone else, our parents, our abuse, whatever is causing all these false starts. We forget that while I was attempting all these new beginnings, I was also pounding a couple of six-packs a night and trying to figure out ways to make money to get cocaine. Working at the local diner wasn't cutting it. I had a job for six months at Mel's Diner in Newton, MA. Mel was a hard-working Italian American father of four children who owned two restaurants. He was the kindest man in the world but very tough. I had to show up to work on time. He wasn't going to put up with my bullshit and eventually fired me.

When I worked at Mel's, I fell for one of the guys who ate breakfast there: Billy with the forearm cross tattoo. He would pull up on his Harley, swagger in, and sit at the counter. I would get goosebumps just being near him. By then, I had done so much cocaine that I had lost some weight and could regularly get dates. Billy asked me to go to a party one night and I was thrilled. He worked at a motorcycle shop and seemed responsible. We began a whirlwind romance of trips on the bike, Laconia weekends, adventures on his enormous waterbed, and more cocaine than you could imagine. Did I mention that he was also a coke dealer?

One small problem with this scenario was that I was living with a guy named Jack. My life became complicated quickly, trying to keep up with the constant lies. I was coming in late, and Jack was starting to get pissed off. It came to a head when one drunken, coke-filled evening Billy and I decided to go to Providence, RI, to get tattoos. We rode his Harley down, hit a couple of bars along the way, and ended up at Joe's Tattoos on Pleasant Street. I was so obsessed with Billy and having such a great time that I decided, with the brilliant thinking of a drunk, that I would get Billy's name tattooed on my lower left bikini line. So I proceeded to get a tattoo that said, "My Star Billy" surrounding a big star. Did I already say I was living with somebody else?

Arriving home that night wasn't pretty. I had a huge bandage on my lower abdomen. I told Jack I had fallen. I'm not sure how one falls on their lower front body, but Jack had a pretty serious drug and alcohol problem, so it took him a while to figure out the lie. One day he saw the tattoo and got enraged. He knew that it was a tattoo (maybe seeing the blue ink sticking out from the bandage?), and ripped the bandage off. This wasn't a good day for me. The next thing I knew, Jack had made plans at a friend's house who was a tattoo artist to get the tattoo covered up.

A month later, in the middle of a snowstorm, Jack dragged me to this guy Wayne's house to get the tattoo "fixed." The big decision was what to choose that would be big enough to cover it. I decided on Pegasus. Maybe I felt like flying away, or perhaps I was so numb and I just didn't care anymore. All I know is getting a tattoo on the lower left quadrant of your stomach hurts like a motherf****r.

During the three hours of feeling like someone was carving into my skin, I felt like I was dreaming. It was taking more and more to get further away from myself—more booze, more drugs, and more boys, which equaled more insanity. The Jack/Billy love triangle got dark toward the end of my using. One night I was sleeping at Billy's house, and in the middle of the night, we were awakened by screaming next door and blue lights flashing outside. Someone was being handcuffed and put into a police cruiser. The following day I got a call from the Newton police station. Jack had tried to hang himself in a cell and was now a patient at Metropolitan State Hospital. The previous evening, Jack had come looking for me at Billy's house but went into the wrong house and woke a couple up while screaming my name. The guilt I felt over hurting him haunted me for a long time.

Soon after this event, I made my last run at trying to get as far away from myself as possible. I longed for a permanent blackout. I wanted to figure out how I could stay at that perfect place all drug addicts want to be: that feeling after the first drink or the first line of coke. "It is impossible to feel 72 degrees and sunny all the time," but we keep trying—over and over and over again. This is not the human condition because feelings come and go, things change. This is one of life's few guarantees. It's a completely unrealistic expectation to think life isn't supposed to be hard.

The final attempt occurred after several incidents where I questioned my sanity. I often felt like I was traveling above my body. Toward the end of my active addiction, I was living at a drug house sporadically. I was now dating a guy named Scotty, who someone said was mixed up with a Mexican drug cartel. I'm not sure if that was true, but Scotty was scary and, of course, he always had lots of cocaine. He had come back into town from Mexico after taking vehicles down there to be sold. Why, you may ask, would I be with this person? My default was that I felt sorry for him. It is the insane conflict of co-crazy. Save them, need them, hate them, use them while simultaneously feeling like a victim.

I was living in Cambridge, MA, with a friend of my brother's in a condo that my cousin owned. I knew the end was closing in and real life was hunting me down. I was somehow still seeing Billy, trying to help Jack, and was now involved with another drug dealer. Shocking. I didn't realize that Scotty was another sociopath that I felt sorry for. One morning as I left my condo, I saw Scotty in a vehicle parked two spaces behind me. I was horrified because I hadn't told him where I lived. He asked me all kinds of questions about where I had been and who I had been with. While I tried to make up lies, I was also trying to accept the overwhelming realization that Scotty was stalking me. I tried to diffuse the situation by telling him to meet me at our mutual friend's house so we could talk.

By this time, I wasn't sure who I owed money to anymore. I began to fantasize about becoming a stripper to make fast money, but I thought I didn't have the body for it. I started to steal things from my family to pay off coke dealers. I began to avoid the people I loved. My parents caring felt like it burned my skin. I knew back in some faraway place in my brain that they loved me and wanted the best for me, but all I could think about was myself and my next high—the selfishness of addiction crowded out any sane thinking.

We all know on some level that we aren't victims and that we are destroying others' lives, but we keep pushing that tidal wave away, and it gets harder and harder to hold it back. I couldn't think about them because the shame and pain and guilt would kill me. Addicts do not want to see their families because it reminds them of their failures and other people's lives moving forward. It is what we are most afraid of. It is what we don't want to face. It is what will break us.

Later that morning, I walked into my friend Gary's house and grabbed a beer from the fridge. It was nine in the morning—cornflakes in a can. I sauntered into the living room. As usual, the residents were taking their blood pressure. Addicts get obsessed with bizarre delusional activities to help us believe that somehow we aren't going to die. We are killing ourselves with drugs and alcohol, but we take our blood pressure so we don't have a heart attack from the coke's speed. I looked around and saw that the room was quiet. Scotty was sitting in a chair in the corner with a nasty look on his face. Oh, crap. He stood up and took his beer and poured it over my head, saying, "I know you cheated on me!" He was right. Although, was I really in a committed relationship with him?

I stood there for about a minute while the beer poured down over my hip rabbit fur jacket. I thought, *Shit, there goes the coat.* On some level, I knew he was right to be angry. He also scared the crap out of me, and I had nothing to say. Gary jumped up and said, "Hey, man, cut it out, that's not okay. Go take a walk."

I'm not sure how the rest of the day went, but I'm sure I took some road to oblivion. I may have gone to a bar. That night, I ended up at Billy's house. Amazing that he still spoke to me with the insanity I brought to his life. But then again, he did deal coke.

Cocaine used to make me feel euphoric for days, but it wasn't working anymore. I could drink a case of beer, smoke ten joints, take a couple of Valiums, and do several grams of coke and be awake for days. It used to make me feel sexy, smart, popular, wanted, and connected. I had this fantasy of living this criminal, fast-lane, extravagant lifestyle, but the truth was I was just an addict chasing the next high. *The problem is you eventually have to come down.*

There is a feeling you get when it is four o'clock in the morning and you have been up for days and nothing is working anymore. It is time for sleep, and a crash begins, where you start to realize what has happened over the previous few days. You remember how you got the money for the drugs, which usually isn't a good memory, and you know that the shame train will be arriving shortly. You begin to assess the damage in your head. Who have I hurt, how much money have I stolen, where did I get it, who did I sleep with, or who did I promise something to?

Waking up in the morning is this slow-motion head shake of trying to get the facts straight in your mind and resisting them at the same time. There is this lightning bolt of fear that shoots through your body before you are fully conscious. Slowly, thoughts and images start to return. You piece together the previous few days as the bits and pieces swirl around, not knowing what is real or imagined. You pray that most of it is imagined. The nauseous feeling in your gut—not from the drugs and booze, but from the awareness of how far down you have gone—isn't going away.

A few days later, I woke up in Billy's apartment on the living room floor after a three-day bender and knew I had gone too far. My body wasn't feeling right. I felt bugs crawling all over me even though there weren't any there. I wondered if I had crossed some line and done a mixture of too many things and had lost my mind. I knew it was going to be over soon because I felt like I was going to die. The fallout from using was getting too great, and the feelings wouldn't stay away. I couldn't escape from myself anymore, and reality was seeping in.

I called my brother Mark. I had partied with him and knew he wouldn't judge me. My oldest brother Will and his wife worked at a psychiatric hospital, and they got me in for treatment within twenty-four hours. This was the beginning of my journey into sobriety, the human race, growing up, having feelings, and getting a life.

8

Waking Up

The first three months of not having anything to take the edge off was like having no skin. Although I was relieved to be alive and not have anything in my system, I was also terrified of being alive and not having anything in my system. Supermarkets overwhelmed me. People made me anxious. Feelings descended upon me like roommates who had been gone for years and suddenly moved back in. Being around my family activated guilt and anxiety, so I only visited as much as my system could tolerate.

As the journey of sobriety began, I went to support meetings constantly. I smoked cigarettes, worked, and drank gallons of coffee. My life was pretty simple and I felt like I had a second chance. I felt blessed. I was grateful. I was terrified. A woman at a meeting once said when she entered recovery, she suddenly woke up and realized she had a husband and four children. I got it. I woke up to a world I didn't recognize and a world I wanted to forget. It was as if I had been floating on this cloud above my life observing what was going on below and suddenly, the cloud dissipated. I fell to earth with no idea where I'd been, what had gone on, or the damage I had done.

The re-entry is like you're recovering from getting zapped by a Taser. Everything mystified me and I felt permanently anxious. Stunned and numbed to life, part of me wanted to come out of it, but at the same time I was ambivalent. There is only so much a system can take before it nearly drowns you in guilt, shame, and remorse.

The universe was taking care of me somehow, letting in small bits of information as I could handle it. The only thing I could think about was not drinking or drugging because anything beyond that was too much. It's hard enough to remember through this foggy state what you have gone through and witnessed, let alone what you have done to others. That part is unbearable. I was now sober and felt like I had missed out and fallen behind in everything. I was twenty-four and completely lost. I felt old. Everything was new. Girls get menstrual cramps. Humans have feelings. Life can be painful. There were disappointments, losses, hurt feelings, and challenges.

There was a slow unfolding of the present and a gradual remembering of the past. Memories of devastation, embarrassment, destruction of relationships, and shameful feelings began to unravel. This miraculously gave way to a subtle, scary joy at being back on the planet, back in relationships, back to awareness of beautiful things. I was becoming more conscious of what was happening around me like an alien who had just landed. I was discovering the thin line between excitement and anxiety, sadness and loss, anger and frustration, and wanting to be present or maybe not.

On the one hand, I wanted life desperately, as if I had been starving for years and now sat at a Las Vegas buffet, and on the other hand, I felt terror at what may be lurking beneath the surface of my heart and mind.

* * *

I returned to college in 1986 with two years of sobriety. I really wanted to be there, unlike my Chicago experience. It was time. I wanted to learn everything. I loved living in Cambridge again and driving into Boston to UMass every day. At one-year sobriety, I bought a Harley-Davidson and rode it down the Southeast Expressway reveling in the new freedom of recovery. I had great friends, I loved going to recovery meetings, and I loved life. I was also moving as if someone was chasing me.

There is a saying in recovery that after the first year, shit starts to get real. Not only are you experiencing joy and participating in life, but memories of the past begin to creep in.

The delicate dance. The dance of allowing the past to move into your consciousness slowly while at the same time not allowing it to come in too fast, leading to overwhelm. Then you want to use. It's a ride on the rollercoaster of expand/restrict, open/close, feel/don't feel, let go/hold on—even live or die.

Three years into recovery, I had an emotional breakdown. I started remembering all this inappropriate sexual behavior of my dad. I had often felt like his wife. Memories were barraging me of feeling held down and restricted. I would be driving home from school and suddenly feel like somebody was holding my wrists. The memory was so strong I would have to pull over. I felt crazy. Real crazy. My body was trying to tell me something. For the next several years, I uncovered many memories of past incidents of violations. Some within the house I was raised and some brought on by my drinking.

I lived in a house where there were no boundaries. It was insidious. A slap on the ass, being emotionally seduced, a pre-occupation with Dad's happiness, my feelings of obligation to him. There was inappropriate touch, too much physical contact, and an expectation for me to meet his emotional needs. I had been trying to grow up and separate. He wanted to hold on tight because if he let go, he may need to face his own harsh reality.

I began regular therapy and group therapy that went on for several years. It uncovered lots of painful crap. If I wanted to move forward with this new dance of my sober life, I had to accept the dips, tolerate the new awareness of my flaws, appreciate the elation of receiving a sixty-day coin, and get up when I fell on my ass. Welcome to recovery.

The patterns I recognized:

• I was beginning to become aware of my desire to not feel.

- I was focused more on others than myself.
- I was having a hard time identifying my feeling states.
- I was compulsively getting into relationships.
- I never felt good enough.
- I needed approval from others.
- I had a hard time speaking up for myself.
- I couldn't even identify what I wanted or needed.

My life was being run by fear and anger and shame. It was playing out in my life everywhere, but I didn't know how much.

When I was in my third year at UMass, I decided to take a trip to a Club Med. I was getting excellent grades and had five years of sobriety, so to celebrate, I went to St. Lucia. My roommate was this wonderful big-boned, life-of-the-party woman from Dallas. It was great to realize I could still have a blast without booze and drugs. Trapezes, snorkeling, gorgeous food, beautiful beaches, sparkling green water, and gratitude for my life filled my heart.

Simultaneously, however, I seemed to keep getting in trouble with men, even when sober. Case in point: I met a lovely young French man, Gabriel, who worked at Club Med, and we had a luscious week-long love affair. He knew how to touch a particular section of a woman's lower back that could bring me to my knees. A couple of weeks after I returned home, I went out with a friend of mine named Tom whom I had met in my recovery meetings. I agreed to go on a date, even though I just wanted to be friends. One of my big issues was that I had a hard time disappointing men and felt terrible that Tom liked me. After the date, when Tom and I returned to my home, he walked me into the screened porch and guess who was sitting there with his bags and a great tan? Gabriel.

In the first five years of my sobriety, I was in a lost adolescence. Not only was I waking up to a sober life, but I was waking up as a woman. I was experiencing new feelings of love, romance, and excitement. My emotions had been repressed for years due to substance abuse. My mother had referred to me as a "late bloomer." Or she would say, "You have such a pretty face." It was always painful to hear. I'd think, "Please just don't say anything."

Now I was this woman in her late twenties making up for lost time but with no clue what I was doing. I was repetitively getting into relationships. I was full of confusion as to how I got there. I actually felt like, *Why is this happening to me?* The girl who never felt wanted was still running the show, although I was entirely unaware of it. It was just like booze and cocaine—nothing is ever enough. I was addicted to everything.

What did I decide to do? Get a doctorate in psychology. I needed to figure this shit out.

I arrived in sunny San Diego in 1991 to attend graduate school feeling like my life had taken on a focus, direction, and purpose. I was still trying to figure myself out. I knew I wanted to help people. I spent an enormous amount of time working on myself because now I would be responsible for helping others resolve their problems. I went to meetings, attended seminars, read books, practiced yoga, and meditated. The struggle to have healthy intimate relationships felt like a far-reaching goal.

When I first moved to California, I felt lucky that I could connect with people at my twelve-step meetings. I hadn't made any close friends yet but became busy with school. After several months of living there, I ended up dating a guy named Joe I'd met at a meeting. Joe had just gotten out of a two-year stint in Folsom for a drug-related crime. I heard him share at a meeting and had the thought, *Wow, he is so authentic, real, and funny—I should go talk to him.* Joe looked like a cartoon character out of a bodybuilding magazine. He was enormous, all muscle and tattoos, and often had a blank stare when I tried to connect with him. Then he would just laugh. He was a sweet person, trying to get his life back together. His parents lived in an affluent section of town and were letting him live there until he got his own place or did something to put him back in prison.

Everyone who is training to be a psychologist is required to participate in their own therapy. Not that I objected. I wanted insight into what had been driving me my whole life. One day, during role playing in a class where we practiced listening skills and validation techniques, I volunteered to be the client, while another student played the therapist. As I sat in the class, discussing my struggles with Joe, the teacher seemed horrified. He said, "Well, sometimes, when people are under stress, they make unusual choices to escape their stress." He had no idea.

I had resolved many issues. I had quit drinking, doing drugs and smoking, and I was gaining awareness and insight into many of my behaviors. But I still felt empty when I wasn't in a relationship and spent too much time seeking one out. There was a low-grade anxiety that would grow into a terror at times when I didn't have a boyfriend or even someone to obsess about. This led to impulsive choices that just enhanced the feeling of loneliness. The pattern became repetitive because I always started dating someone whom I was physically attracted to but then realized after a couple of months that we didn't have anything in common. Not that this always stopped me.

I came to realize that I didn't just want a sexual relationship. Initial attraction is fun but it has nothing to do with personality or whether or not he or she is right for you. I was tired of choosing the wrong people but struggled with waiting to be physical. The longer I stayed sober, the more I saw my behaviors with men did not get me what I wanted. If I could hold off on sex, I could get to know someone and save myself and others trouble and heartache. This skill, when utilized, ended a lot of potential relationships after about three weeks. Their physical appeal would fade fast when I got beyond that initial la la land stage. It is amazing who people turn out to be if you can get beyond that first endorphin buzz.

I continued to work on myself—the personal relationships got better and better. My choices improved and I picked emotionally healthier people. I was still learning how to figure out the unconscious motives, unresolved pieces of my history, buried feelings, and the relentless desires to escape that were driving my behavior.

Could I learn to tolerate uncomfortable feelings? I continued to see the power of the emotions I was running from—the fear of not being wanted, the fear of not being loved, and the fear of not being enough, not to mention an untapped rage about being a woman. Those feelings drove me, made decisions for me, skewed my perception of reality, and made me say yes when I wanted to say no. When I was in the middle of trying to figure all this out, I met Shane.

9

More Crazy

I met Shane while in my final year of graduate school. I was enjoying a veggie sandwich at a health food restaurant on the ocean in Del Mar, and a man was sitting alone across from me peeking over his book. We caught one another's eye and began discussing the book he was reading on a particular therapy.

Shane told me he had owned and sold an advertising company in Vancouver, Canada, and that for the past two years he'd been traveling around the world. When I met him, he was living in a blue van he called "The Womb." He had traveled up and down the California coast, staying at ashrams, attending yoga retreats and healing workshops. He was trying to find himself. Shane told me a long tale of addiction, recovery, divorce, and an ex-wife with MS. Along the way he had found his biological mother after a long search, and then was rejected by her again. Lots of trauma and woundedness.

He was perfect.

Shane and I had a whirlwind romance. He settled back in Vancouver, and I flew up from San Diego for romantic weekends and blissful connections. For two years, we were both captivated by the emotional rollercoaster of a long-distance relationship and my insanity of wanting him to be the one. The tick of my biological clock was deafening. I was thirty-

CO-CRAZY REMINDER

When they say their truth, believe it.
When there are red flags, see them.
When you feel a conflict inside, recognize it.

seven years old, wanted to have children, and dreamed of that magical wedding.

To complicate matters, I received a terrific job offer at a hospital in Boston. We decided to move across the country and start our life together. For the first time in years, I would be living with someone. I was ready to start my career as a psychologist but was also leaving my friends and support system in California. Shane would be leaving his country, his friends, his connections, and had no idea what he wanted to do with his life. Moreover, I would be living near my father for the first time in six years. I thought to myself, *What could possibly go wrong?*

We rented a house an hour outside of Boston and I started my career as a psychologist. One minute I felt like I couldn't live without him, and the next minute I wanted to kill him. I often felt like I was losing my mind when I would try to communicate with Shane. I would get so frustrated and consumed with how *he* was feeling, I would lose my own ground. He was exploring a lot, trying to find his place in a new country, and his own trauma was being activated because of it. It was intense all the time. It was either really good or really, really bad.

Love is about bringing the best out of your partner, not the worst (at least not that frequently). I felt so lucky at times. I thought that I had met the most amazing man in the world, but simultaneously I struggled with chronic self-doubt. This was only the second time I had lived with someone in sobriety. I realized I was in constant fear of him leaving, but I didn't want to give up the fantasy of the happy couple. I couldn't see my own selfishness of wanting what I wanted without considering the effects on others. I was driven to fulfill a fantasy, so I ignored the voice inside due to the fear of failing at something I waited so long to do.

Even though we were both sober, it was like living with active addiction. Crazy and co-crazy. Shane would suffer deep, intense depressions, and I was in a state of chronic frustration. I wanted peace and happiness, but I was living with someone who was in constant crisis. One minute he wanted me and the next minute he couldn't make up his mind. Just when I'd feel safe in the relationship (every three months or so), he would say something like, "I may need to go to Sweden for a while because I think I have some unfinished business with a woman there."

OMG. What the f**k?!

It was not just about Shane's behaviors. My own mental health was deteriorating. I wanted this relationship, but on some deeper level, I knew it wasn't right. I'm sure he felt the same way. We weren't a match. Due to both of us having had a series of unsuccessful relationships, we wanted to make this one work. We had a deep connection, and at the same time, our personalities were nothing alike. I began to get more and more anxious and depressed. I was frustrated and angry, and all my energy was put into dealing with my relationship anxieties. I felt lost in the relationship.

Shane and I had gone to a Catholic pre-marriage weekend where couples learn about love and marriage. We did guided exercises on how we felt about family, money, commitment, children, health, and work. By the end of the weekend, the priest who led the workshop asked us if we really thought we should get married. Everyone could see our incompatibility but us. Despite the warning, we ended up getting married. We honestly tried to make our marriage work. We did another couples relationship weekend on communication. We also went to couple's therapy. I remember going to his therapist with him and bringing a list five pages long of the things Shane didn't like about me. The therapist said, "Criticism kills relationships." All the signs were there. We did have a fantastic wedding. A wedding, however, does not make a marriage.

The First Big Shift: My Co-Crazy Bottom with Max

My son, Max, was three months old. I hadn't had a good night's sleep in six months due to stomach and bladder problems during my pregnancy, and I was also experiencing some waves of post-partum. All I wanted was to keep my baby safe and take care of him. At the same time, I was out of my mind. I was depressed, overwhelmed, lost and scared. I was slowly awakening to the fact that I had no idea how to be a mother. Shane seemed upset and angry all the time. I needed him to help me but I was afraid to ask. I wondered, "What can I do to make him happier—is it possible?" I also felt sorry for him. Did I somehow do this to him?

I took a maternity leave, so I had six months at home with Max. I had fantasized about the beginning of motherhood being this beautiful, intimate time with my husband, sharing the magic of caring for a new life. The first few months of Max's life were physically and emotionally grueling. I felt the isolation, the lack of sleep, the problems in the marriage, the low self-esteem, anxiety, perfectionism and the delusion that everyone else knew how to do this but me. I became obsessed with two books on parenting. I read them over and over again. I followed every single instruction. I was so relieved that someone knew what they were doing.

I told myself, "You're doing a good job." I was proud of myself when I developed a sleep schedule for Max. He finally began sleeping through the night. I got a light feeling that I may be okay. I was in a mother's group, but I couldn't relate to anyone. They were talking about car seats and recipes and the latest tip on child-rearing, and my marriage was imploding. Shane was unhappy, but I didn't know how to fix it. I was angry that I felt like I had to fix it.

Intermittently, the awareness would surface that my marriage might not work out. I realized that when we were dating, I could focus on him, adore him and listen to his brilliant ideas. I felt so desperate not to lose his love but now there was something way more significant occupying every moment. I was responsible for another human being. I couldn't stroke Shane's ego anymore.

I also couldn't take the criticisms. It felt relentless. For example, I'm not a vegetarian. Shane knew this, but I kept trying to please him by trying to find a happy middle ground for what I ate. He became furious one day when he found Burger King wrappers in my car. I was just trying to get through the day and he was worried that I was eating meat. We could not communicate. Shane was like a restless animal trying to escape. At the same time, he was terrified, just like me. We were both wounded individuals before we met and had no emotional tools to navigate this new road. He wasn't doing well either, but I wanted him to step up to the plate. I didn't have the energy to take care of him. I couldn't be his shrink. I was resentful that he had needs when I was barely functioning.

One morning, I was upstairs changing my son's diaper, getting him ready for the day. I was wrapping him in a blanket, and I saw blotches of blood on my son's skin. The more I moved him to search for the source, the more it spread. I picked him up and ran downstairs and started screaming at my husband, "What did you do to him?!" He yelled, "I didn't do anything, what are you talking about!?" We put Max down and frantically kept looking, and suddenly, Shane stops and looks up at me. It felt like we were frozen in time, our faces stuck staring at each other, hearing our breathing in the silence. Then he says, "You cut your finger."

At that moment, I realized I had cut my finger before I went to get Max. I hadn't noticed it, so every time I moved him, and tried to find the problem, the blood kept spreading. A more significant realization was seeping through the fog of my depression and exhaustion. Standing in that silent moment was the awareness that I thought my husband had hurt our son. There was no coming back from this. Shane moved out. I had hit bottom with co-crazy.

This was the first of two emotional bottoms of co-crazy. This one was due to the perfect storm of circumstances in my relationship with Shane. The second came years later in another perfect storm during my second marriage. After this incident with Shane, I knew I had to surrender. I could not fix this on my own, which was exactly how it had been with my addictions. There is a progression of co-crazy, like with any addiction. It keeps getting worse and worse and the costs keep getting higher and higher. The circumstances are different because a person is the substance that we use, but the feelings of fear, resignation, anger, and shame are all the same.

What we are using to ameliorate our past histories—our rage, our fear, our pain, our lives' situations—is no longer working. Whether it is busyness, avoidance, over-functioning, drinking, or shooting heroin, these are all ways to escape the truth of what we feel, what we think, and who we are. I no longer was using drugs, but I had a compulsive need to be in relationships. This unconscious fear of facing everything had propelled me into this present situation. When I stopped long enough to feel or think, I knew I had created all of it. How could I stop this destructive pattern of relating?

It was time to start digging deeper through the consciousness called Sarah. Again. I needed some courage and strength.

Help me, God, find peace.
Guide me, Lord.
Heal my body, mind and heart.
Give me patience.
Fill me with your spirit.
Let me be the love.

When we are in relationships, our deepest fears and our most intense anger become activated. Our feelings of loss, love, pain, horror, and bliss can all be felt on some soul level when we are in a relationship, and especially when we are *losing* a relationship. Besides feeling like I was unraveling, having a baby continued to motivate me to heal because co-crazy can be in any relationship. I knew that if I was going to be a good parent, I had to recognize my issues that could get triggered by mothering. This was going to be one of the most important relationships in my life. I did not want to pass my own childhood wounds onto my son—there was no way I was going to let that happen.

I knew I needed to go back and look at the dynamics learned with my parents and how those affected my subsequent patterns with men. I was now responsible for another human being. A boy no less. It was the most significant responsibility I would ever have. Two things were happening. I needed to learn how to co-parent with Shane, which meant healing old relational wounds, *and* I needed to learn how to be a mother, which meant healing old relational wounds. *Great.*

Becoming a mother changed everything. I know if you are reading this book and have children, you know this. I no longer had that intense longing for a man to fill my soul. I also knew it was not my son's job to fill my emptiness. When I had Max, I was responsible for his life. I did not want to screw that up. My problems were exacerbated when I became a mother, and I had no idea that my unresolved crap would be coming out on my partner. It is the way it is—there is no denying this axiom. The good news is that having a child is an exceptional opportunity to see your bad behaviors and change them. Take the opportunity to get to know yourself and begin to have an awareness of these dynamics. It will save you so much time later on. (Suspend your disbelief for now.) Taking responsibility will lead to freedom.

Everything that comes out of our mouths is about us, not the child. We are responsible for what we say, how we act, and what we project onto them. Parenting is about the parents. If you can start there, your kids will be fine. If our fear and anger are running our lives, then we will continuously put our anxieties, projections, and feelings onto our children. People don't *make* us do anything, not even a whiny child. We make choices. I'm not going to get into a big debate here, so try to trust me. Forgive yourself right now for whatever you have done and start now. It is never too late. False mommy guilt paralyzes us. Forget it.

After this first emotional bottom, I saw how my behaviors in that relationship didn't work. I had to start again with my emotional recovery. I had to accept and surrender to what was happening right now. No fantasy. No escape. Just acknowledge reality. This was my starting point. Start exactly where you are. No judgment, no shame, just breathe. What needs to happen now in this crisis? Yes, you will be feeling feelings, but is there some small action you can take? Do it. Do one thing.

I began by attending a twelve-step program for families because I heard this was where I would learn to have healthy relationships. *Do you think I wanted to go?* No, of course not. I was desperate and willing to do what anyone told me to do. Denial is a powerful thing. It inhibits awareness and action. It was time for more truth. Not for the truth about what happened to me but the truth about what I had created. How was I a part of what I created? I was responsible for my *response* to life. Moreover, at the cellular level, I knew in my heart that if I didn't resolve my emotional crap, it would come out on my boy. The passing on of generational pathology had to stop with me. I did not want him to grow up in crazy.

My co-parenting role with Shane was an enormous opportunity to practice not reacting. Being a working mother was great practice for having feelings. I also had a job as a psychologist at a psych hospital, which helped me to grow up, be responsible, and become an example and not a problem. The big shift: Moving from thinking it is about everyone else to *knowing* it is about me = the beginning of the healing of co-crazy.

* * *

It would be ridiculous to say that I hadn't done any previous work on myself. I knew on some level that I was responsible for the problems in my life, but this was a new level of knowledge. It culminated perhaps from doing all the emotional work of therapy and getting sober, or being tired of the drama with men, or becoming a new mother. These moments of enormous psychological and emotional distress can feel like your life is ending, and in some way it is. The person I had known had to change and become someone new. It was an ending and a new beginning; another transformation was taking place. The times of the most considerable pain can often be the times of great healing.

I wanted to be a mother that Max could admire and respect, to start living life from a place of empowerment, not of desperation. I wanted freedom. I had to up my recovery game. I was responsible for how another human being felt about themselves. I wanted the freedom to feel okay within myself. Freedom to love everyone just the way they are. Freedom to not take things personally and to see the bigger picture beyond just myself.

I wanted to be a loving contributor to life. I wanted to be a vessel for the universal spirit to work through me and guide me to what was right. No more blocks to the sunlight of the spirit. Freedom. What would I do? I needed to have the strength of a warrior to surrender and cope with the crazy. These were my commitments. Think about which ones you want to take on:

- I'm responsible for my happiness.
- I will start telling myself the truth about who I am, what I've done, what I've experienced, my history, and my behavior.
- No more running, no more escaping through using relationships to not focus on myself.
- I will not get stopped by my feelings; they are just feelings, clouds passing by (sometimes with intense bodily sensations).
- I will heal the shame of my relationship and sexual history.
- I will forgive myself.
- I will stop being run by fear and anger.
- I can start getting comfortable with powerlessness over other people.
- I am not in charge—God is.

Leaving Crazy Town

Take Action: Decide to save your own life. Nothing changes if nothing changes.

I went to a seminar once where the seminar leader said to think about going up to a mountain top and screaming all our thoughts, feelings, and opinions as loud as we could up to the stars. He said, "That's about how much the universe is affected by your thoughts and feelings." Brutal. His point was the thing that makes the most difference is action. If we want to change, we have to take responsibility for those changes. If we want our lives to become more manageable, peaceful, and joyful, we will need to get moving. We can't just talk about something forever and think it will change, especially when trying to get someone else to change.

Change can initially be painful. I wish this weren't the case. Willingness won't arrive until we are in enough pain. Some of the most painful changes I had to make have involved knowing that someone else was going to get hurt. I've been divorced twice. I loved both of those men. I also knew I was dying inside. If I stayed in those relationships, I would have gotten worse and worse and eventually would have completely lost myself. The concept of how I wanted my life to be and the actual reality of my life was not lined up.

For me to face this reality, I had to acknowledge my unhappiness and that I didn't have all the answers. I had to trust that life could get better and know that the change was up to me. I needed to find the courage to say to myself, "This is not working out" and do something different. The loss of a relationship and the loss of the fantasy of a family had to be accepted and let go. The vision of a little family, all smiles, having a barbecue with friends was not going to be my reality. Saving my own life had to be more important than hurting someone's feelings. It had to be.

Leaving Crazy Town

Stop "Checking Out"

Partial list: Alcohol, drugs, gambling, food, sex, shopping, a person, distraction, the phone. You get the idea.

This is the thing: you can't change any of the other behaviors in your life until you accept this one truth. The brutal reality is that if you continue to be in denial about your problems, you will create more drama, regrets, insanity, and broken relationships. Does getting clean and sober suck at first? It might. Try to get it in your head somehow: the denial around the addiction/other person or other issue is the quintessential component of keeping it alive. Our minds tell us we don't have it. Again, *it tells you that you don't have it.* Two words: mental illness. Denial is a killer.

All I know is, if you can stop lying to yourself, you might have a chance. Try to face some facts about your life. I would tell you to ask your girlfriend or boyfriend, but I have had spouses tell me everything is just fine because they are in denial too. For those of you who are thinking, *Oh, I'm not an addict,* to be clear, I'm not just talking about substances you ingest. It is not just about substances, right? Anything you are using right now that keeps you separate from yourself and others is something you may be in denial about.

- Something that people around you complain about.
- Something that you feel guilty or ashamed about— maybe even self-hatred.
- Something you may be obsessed with and keep trying to change.
- Something that causes you distress.
- Something that you have to keep rationalizing to make it okay for you to keep doing.
- Something that is no longer working but you can't stop.
- Something that has become a much more significant part of your life than you want.

CO-CRAZY REMINDER

If you can get help and quit the substances, you can address the co-crazy. Your life will continue to improve, you will get connected to others in an authentic way, and things you never thought possible will happen. You do not have to continue to be in pain, guilt, and remorse about using, whatever that may be. There is a beginning, middle, and an end to getting sober—once you decide to put it down. If you don't quit? Things will progressively get worse. That is an absolute guarantee.

What makes any addiction worse is it may take a while to finally stop. It may be a long slow slog of progression where for years your addiction gets worse and gets in the way of your life over and over again, but you spend your whole life in this semi-conscious state. You'll be putting out fires left and right while living a life of utter mediocrity and pain. I am so grateful for crashing and burning early so I could then recreate my life.

Don't waste your life in Numbland.

Your life can transform. I promise.

Clients who weren't ready to quit never come back five years later and tell me things got better. It does not happen. Quite the opposite is true.

If your life is unraveling because of another obsession or preoccupation, find help to put it down. Figure out a plan. Talk to somebody. The first step in healing from any addiction or co-crazy behavior is just to acknowledge it exists. The ownership of the problem is the first step to healing. In twelve-step programs, they call this "a bottom," but you can hit this experience and feeling in all kinds of ways. Ask yourself if you are suffering, and spend a lot of time trying to rationalize your behavior.

The cognitive defense of denial makes it challenging to figure out addictions with your own brain. Sometimes sitting down with someone and looking at the facts helps. Facts don't lie. Sometimes when a client has come to see me for a substance

CO-CRAZY REMINDER

One step at a time, one day at a time, and sometimes, one moment at a time. You can do this.

abuse issue, they think it is about everything else but the addiction. They want to talk about their job, wife, kids, life's dramas, and friends who don't listen, etc. They see the substance as the one thing holding them together. Drug and alcohol abuse are presented as no big deal, even though it's killing them.

Deep down inside, we know. Somewhere in our consciousness there is this awareness that we need to quit using, look at a particular behavior, or stop acting out. The denial stops working, and it becomes hard to rationalize why our lives aren't going as we planned. There is suddenly a little crack in the armor that light can get through. It is scary to think about stopping the only thing we believe has been saving our life.

There is also the fear of what comes afterward. On some level, we know we have been coping with certain intolerable situations by checking out with a substance or a substitute. Will it mean I have to get divorced, or quit the job I hate, or confront my painful past, or discipline my kids who are driving me nuts? Maybe. But this is all on your timetable. First, save your life and stop trying to manage everything. When you are clear minded and have support, it gets easier. Nothing outside yourself will change until you handle this part. The addiction is just a symptom of underlying causes and conditions, so give yourself a break; it does not all have to happen at once.

Leaving Crazy Town

Ask for Help

Self-reliance is a brilliant skill to learn while growing up. We learn how to take care of ourselves and be independent but one of the consequences is that we have a heck of a time asking for help when we need it. People ask us if we need anything and before they even get the words out, we say, "No, I'm okay" or the classic "I'm fine."

FINE acronym: *F***ed up, Insecure, Neurotic and Emotional or Feelings Inside Not Expressed.*

Even if we are not okay, these expressions become our permanent responses. We may decide at a young age that we are better off relying on ourselves due to a variety of circumstances. It all comes down to how we interpreted our environments throughout our lives and the meanings we attached to those interpretations.

Sometimes, as kids, we can interpret a benign event or interaction as something utterly different than how the person meant it. A client once told me that he always had the belief, "I'm a burden to my mother, and she doesn't love me" due to one incident that he misinterpreted profoundly. It impacted his life in a way in which he became self-reliant and had challenges seeing others as wanting to help him.

When he was about seven years old, he came home from school, excited about a project he had finished. He couldn't wait to show it to his mom, but when he got back home, his mom was at the stove cooking and was busy with her two other children. He kept trying to get her attention to get her to look at his project. She got angry and told him to go to his room and that she didn't have time to look at it right then. I'm sure other hurts or rejections happened in his life to confirm a belief he then framed about himself—that he was a burden to his mother. Which unfortunately can then generalize to "I'm a burden to everyone."

We can create long-standing beliefs about others and ourselves because of one interpretation. We end up not wanting to risk being disappointed or hurt, and we don't want to feel rejected if we reach out for help. As adults, we then take things personally rather than remind ourselves that others' availability or unavailability to help is not about us. Don't make up a story about it; just ask someone else. Ask until you get the help you need and deserve.

I remember a friend of mine saying to me once, "If you say you don't need help all the time, you don't allow the other person to feel how *you* feel when you're helping someone. . . . Don't rip that person off of having that feeling because of your fear." Ouch. Wow. I love helping people. So why would I not let someone feel good if they could help me? I often hear a client say, "Well, I made the call and asked someone for help, and they couldn't do it." Okay, but what about trying someone else? That doesn't have to be the end of the road! Don't give up. People want to help.

I have a brother who is one of the most self-reliant people I know. He is a loving, kind, caring, would-do-anything-for-you kind of guy. I think he built his barn by himself. He only got help when a wall needed to be pulled up. It isn't good or bad. Our original environment decided for us when we were two or three years old that these folks who were supposed to be taking care of us were a bit preoccupied with themselves, so we had to learn to wing it.

I had a brilliant, extremely self-reliant client once who wrote her entire fourth step in Alcoholics Anonymous by herself. I said, "Don't you think you needed a sponsor to do that?" She just laughed.

THOSE F***ING THOUGHTS AND FEELINGS: Working with the Core of Co-Crazy

"You know you're co-crazy when
you fall off a cliff and someone
else's life flashes before your eyes."

—Anonymous

10

Being Human = Having Feelings

The ironic thing about recovery from anything is that we are all trying to get back to being human. We can witness freedom watching a child living in the moment, feeling and expressing themselves fully. One minute they are crying, the next minute they're frustrated, and then the minute after that, they're laughing. They aren't attached to any of it or making up significant meanings or creating rigid belief systems. They flow from one thing to the next, free in their being. They are in the present.

As we grow older and experience a disappointment, an upset, a hurt, a disillusionment, a rejection, or an abandonment, we start laying the armor on, piece by piece, to hold ourselves together. If we are lucky we may get to therapy, or we get sober or begin to attend another twelve-step program where we are given permission to feel our feelings. It takes time, but the armor will begin to fall to the ground.

When I got sober, my first challenge was to start getting comfortable with having feelings. The problem was feelings would come at me like a sandstorm, and the intensity would barrage my body like sand whipping through me. I'd even find it hard to breathe sometimes. One example of this was when

I was supposed to get together with my sponsor for the first time. She called that morning and couldn't make it. Hearing the news, I proceeded to throw myself onto my bed, sobbing with my arm over my eyes like a teenager after a breakup. My sponsor was sick. That was it. I hadn't felt disappointment, or sadness, or much of anything but numbness and detachment for a long time. This out-of-proportion reaction was the beginning of feelings coming back into my own body.

Part of the process of coming back into your body is learning how to identify feeling states. It sounds elementary, but many of us spend a lifetime trying *not* to feel. I have met many people over the years who can't identify their feelings. We use all kinds of methods and distractions not to feel. Early in sobriety, an incident would happen and five days later, I would have the feeling related to the event. It took a long time to get the event and the feeling to happen simultaneously. I was slowly allowing my body to experience life.

For example, I would get off the phone with my dad. I would feel "off" but not know why. Within twenty-four hours of the phone call, I would begin to notice bizarre behaviors:

- Suddenly an ice-cream sundae was a great idea.
- A boyfriend was needed immediately.
- I found myself at a movie theater all afternoon watching three movies in a row.
- A day later, I might feel a panic attack coming on.
- I inexplicably felt sad.
- I felt like I needed to run to a twelve-step meeting.

Then four days later, I would be in a therapy session and say, "I'm so mad at what my dad said on the phone the other day." Unfamiliar territory. It was a process of starting to get more comfortable with tolerating and identifying feeling states. I had to remember that the feeling would not kill me, even though sometimes it felt that way. The actions one takes to avoid feelings are what can kill us. Insert your favorite escape here.

So the first step is just to identify: What is the feeling? Now what? Holy crap, now I have to sit with it. You begin to realize that emotions pass if we don't make up a big story about them, and you let them flow through. That's it. What we resist, persists. Symptoms become more lethal when we intentionally or unintentionally avoid unpleasant feelings. Then all hell can break loose. It can be a relapse, an affair, an anger outburst, a panic attack, a depression—anything to move away from our underlying feeling states. It's nobody's fault. This is the way we learned to deal, or not deal with feelings. Eventually we realize our ways of coping with feelings doesn't serve us—avoiding stops serving us, acting out doesn't work anymore, and our relationships suffer because of it. We are often left having to address the crisis we created to avoid feelings rather than just feel them.

Over the years, I have seen many ways that clients avoid the truth about themselves by not allowing feelings to surface. I knew a woman who every time she got six months of sobriety, she relapsed. It happened four times in a row until we identified what had happened. What was she avoiding facing or feeling? What revealed itself was that by six months of sobriety, she couldn't tolerate her husband's demeaning tone anymore. Unconsciously, she was terrified about facing her marriage, speaking up for herself, dealing with conflict, and the possibility of divorce, so she drank again. Staying focused on her drinking was more comfortable than confronting years of built-up anger. She couldn't face the pain of her feelings of invisibility and never feeling validated by her husband.

Another example is a mother who was focused on her daughter's athletics, grades, successes, and failures so she didn't have to deal with her own life. She had suffered severe depression for years. Rage and terror were her two operating systems. Feelings were like a dark tunnel she didn't want to enter. She feared that if she went in, she might never come out. Her husband was verbally abusive, she hated her job, and her daughter was not the success that she needed to elevate her own self-esteem. Growing up, her own mother had controlled her with guilt and buying her gifts. Facing the truth about herself may have meant making significant changes. Denying her feelings and staying busy kept her rage at a distance for a long time. People avoid awareness of feeling states because it may mean they have to take action. They assume change is risky—but that is not necessarily true.

Dealing with feelings can feel tortuous to people at first. It's hard to look at yourself and face the truth without judgment. The key is treating yourself with kindness and compassion. Ask yourself, "How would I treat my closest friend if they were struggling to face their feelings about something?" I hope you would say, "I would be kind and listen and love her." Exactly.

That's what is required of you when you are beginning to open up to your feelings and your truth. There is a good reason why we avoid feelings—they can be painful. But real ease, freedom, and liberation come when we can become more present and more willing to even just notice our feelings. There is a release in our body and in our beings. There is a new awareness of "I made it," "It didn't kill me," and "I'm okay."

It is empowering to learn to identify, feel, and express your feelings. You don't need to live in fear of your own human experience. It's happening anyway! People will go to great lengths to hide from themselves, but true peace comes from the acceptance of one's feelings, no matter what they are.

It isn't just avoiding feelings. We are also unaware that our emotions run our lives. Repressing or overreacting are two extremes of the same thing. Both are responses to fear. Sometimes it may be feeling as if the only options are silence or screaming, but taking your feelings out on other people never works. The feelings are inside you. Somebody just pushed the right button. You can get better at identifying and tolerating feelings rather than externalizing your fear and taking them out on your loved ones. We can sometimes have agendas for the people around us and not even know it. We want people to act in a certain way, and if they don't, we get angry. Co-crazy. We can't understand that the other person is having their own experience. They are almost always *not* trying to hurt us on purpose.

A great example of this scenario was when my son was a

senior in high school. Different agendas happening at the same time often lead to explosive interactions. I was grateful for some co-crazy recovery under my belt by this point.

Max walked through the door.

Max: "Mom, can I talk to you?"

Me: "Sure, what's going on?"

Max: "I'm seriously considering joining the military after graduation."

First of all, there is nothing wrong with joining the military. However, my body silently went into convulsions while visions of my son's bloody body on a battlefield flashed before me. What I really wanted to do was scream, "Are you f***ing kidding me?" My mind was going crazy, and my co-crazy head voice was flipping like windshield wipers on high-speed wanting me to tell him what to do and control him.

My head voice was screaming inside: How could you break my heart, how could you do this to me? Haven't I brought you up right? I want you to go to college! You know how I feel about war! What did I do wrong? When did I lose you? Oh my God. This must be his father, I'm going to kill that guy, I thought you wanted to be a psych major—blah, blah, blah.

At that moment, I remembered a line from one of my twelve-step programs: "Pause, when agitated or doubtful." That phrase has saved my life many times.

At that moment with Max, the words that came out of my mouth were given to me by grace beyond me: I simply said, "Okay, tell me about it."

I listened to my son's thoughts. I validated his feelings. I noticed my fear and I was aware of my intense bodily sensations. I gave Max room to investigate this path. I did not resist. *I cared more about the relationship itself rather than being right.* I cared more about his need to communicate than my agenda for his future. Eventually, I got him together with a psychiatrist colleague who had been in the army. We all went out to dinner and got more information. My son decided against it. It was his own decision.

We did not have to get in a power struggle because of *my* feelings, because my reactions were not about him. It was all me. That is the thing with feelings. If we can train ourselves to own them, be responsible for them, and not act out on them, our relationships will improve significantly. I'm not perfect, and it's never easy but it is always worth it.

Tips for Working with Feelings

- No judgments when it comes to having feelings; just notice what's happening.

- Remember human beings have feelings. We are not robots!

- Practice just acknowledging your feeling experiences throughout the day. Some people set a timer every couple of hours to check in with themselves and practice identifying how they feel.

- If you want to begin to identify and experience feelings, practice delaying your typical avoidance or detachment techniques, even for five or ten minutes.

- Practice meditation (yes, I said it) even for five minutes a day. Sit with yourself and notice what's there.

Questions to Dive Deeper

1. Think about how you are expressing yourself. Do you overreact? Withhold?

2. How do you relate to feelings? Avoid, repress, deny, distract, use addictions?

3. What are underlying beliefs about having feelings in general?

It is so important to begin to get comfortable with experiencing feelings because your feelings can profoundly affect your relationships. End the pattern of reacting out of locked-up feelings from the past. Learn to identify what they are really about and where the intensity originated. If you are experiencing a severe bodily and emotional response while having feelings, just breathe and remember it will pass eventually. You are okay. The goal here is to have healthy relationships, which requires being able to acknowledge, identify, then express your feelings so they aren't running your life.

11

Anger

Jane: *"Have you thought about therapy?"*
Skye: *"No, but I've thought about revenge."*

Unresolved anger is one of the quintessential ingredients of peoples' lack of peace and one of the main underlying issues in addiction and co-crazy. Anger can be an ever-present dominating force within these relationships. When we are stuck waiting for someone to change, we are in a chronic state of frustration. There is no freedom when you are unaware that you are spending most of your time trying to escape an underlying experience of anger and resentment. Peoples' pasts play out in their present lives, whether they know it or not.

My clients would continuously illustrate examples of acting out one's anger. One client "forgot" to pick her husband up at the airport. It turned out she had buried rage because he hadn't called during his entire vacation with his buddies. Unconscious anger can play out in endless ways including emotional unavailability, overeating, not eating, speaking too much, not speaking, not being able to connect with people, even needing to be funny. I've had many female clients who found it difficult to make female friends because of old unconscious resentments toward adolescent girlfriends who betrayed them. Anger significantly affects our relationships.

The unbelievable thing about repressed anger and the underlying fears is that it perpetuates our behaviors daily. We think we actively have control over our lives and choices but don't realize that our past is still running us. We aren't in control of it at all. I remember attending the est seminars back in the '80s. I loved them because of the clarity I got around the idea of being run by our past. I remember a seminar leader saying one time, "If you don't figure out why you are doing some of your behaviors, you are taking your past, lobbing it into your future, and just living into your history, over and over again." If we don't resolve the resentments from our earlier lives, we will keep acting out this unresolved anger in all our relationships.

Ninety-five percent of the time you feel a wave of intense anger, it has nothing to do with the present moment.

Anger can be tricky because some folks are aware of their anger but unaware of the underlying reason for it. Anger is often a way we cope with underlying feelings of anxiety, fear, or hurt. When something happens, and I feel an intense energy in my chest and impulsively want to lash out at someone, this anger is not about the present situation. This phenomenon is apparent when there is an incongruence between the event and the reaction. When I get a coffee at Dunkin' Donuts and the server forgets my cream, and I completely lose it, it is not about the coffee.

When I would get angry, my line to myself eventually became "not about now" because I had started to believe that my anger was mainly about earlier experiences of fear and powerlessness that were getting activated. We can disguise anger in numerous ways, so this was a helpful way to work with it. I visualized anger as a five-leveled pyramid. At the top of the pyramid (level 5) is Rage, including explosiveness and uncontrolled acting out; underneath that is Anger, which includes agitation, irritability, restlessness, angst, and anxiety. Beneath that is Sadness, and that includes fatigue, depression, loneliness. Next is Fear, and at the very bottom (level 1) of the pyramid is Powerlessness.

When we have an anger response, earlier wounds, hurts, fears, or experiences of shame, guilt, or powerlessness can come alive. This happened to me regularly when dealing with my ex-husband. When I was dealing with Shane, it was an enormous opportunity to resolve some old anger. Shane could say a couple of words to begin a sentence and I would erupt inside. Not about Shane. Remember, I had told myself that I did not want any anger coming out in my relationship with my son, so I knew I had to look at this.

Just looking at Shane upset me. He would make a particular noise or say, "Hi" on the phone and I would be enraged. Insane? Yes. The classic definition of insanity is when we continue to do the same thing over and over expecting a different result. It is part of the co-crazy dynamic where I'm blaming him for my anger and wanting him to change, but I'm the one who's suffering! After repeatedly responding to him by either getting upset, crying, or hanging up, I realized that this way of relating wasn't working for either of us. How I was acting toward my ex-husband was an excellent example of how unresolved anger was running my life. I was angry every time I talked to this person but he was just being himself. To clarify, this is not to minimize or deny that Shane may have a personality that sometimes comes across as condescending. However, I was losing my peace of mind by giving Shane power over my feelings. My happiness was in Shane's hands. Sound familiar?

The anger was inside of me. Shane could unknowingly affect whether I had a good or bad day because I was reacting to something he did or said. He had a certain tone that I heard as demanding. It was as if he was telling me what was going to happen, rather than asking. This often triggered rage that masked my feelings of powerlessness and my feeling of being misunderstood. I had a reaction to him that I don't have with other people. The situation felt somehow familiar. It reminded me of someone from the past. Shane and I had a long history to work through, but we could only get to resolutions when we both took responsibility for our anger and stopped blaming the other.

Over time, repressed anger becomes an accumulation of resentments, wounds, and disappointments. It manifests in how we behave in our relationships and how intensely we react to things. We become walking resentment factories acting out our anger on all our loved ones by either externalizing our anger or internalizing it by shutting down or detaching. The source of it all is our history, which we carry around like superhero shields. We think that our anger is protecting us and keeping us safe, but instead it perpetuates our fear, keeps us alone, in conflict with everyone or living a life like an actor in a play completely detached from self.

The source of my anger that perpetually came out in my intimate relationships was connected to my repressed rage toward my dad. In intimate relationships, I would become emotionally unavailable, I'd stay busy, or I'd use a variety of other coping tools to avoid dealing with my rage. To get clarity as to why I was so angry, I had to figure out what button was pushed from the past regarding Dad. This would happen regularly when I became reactive with Shane.

As a child I felt responsible for my father's happiness and felt controlled by him, which led to a crippling fear of upsetting people—manifesting as the relentless low-grade chronic hum of anxiety. I had a fear that I couldn't control other people's feelings *and* a fear of looking at what my feelings were. The fear was what was underneath my anger. How could I be myself in a relationship when I was relentlessly trying to manage myself and my partner to avoid feelings, especially anger and fear?

Due to my level of fear, I often chose people I believed I could control, but this was a delusion. I picked men whom I saw as caring, smart, successful, thoughtful, emotionally available, and funny, but underneath I needed them to need me. I confused love with need, so I was recreating old patterns, trying to gain mastery over the past by how I behaved in my new relationship.

My first husband used to say to me, "You are so angry," and I would feel perplexed. What does he mean I'm angry? That is the complexity of relationships and anger. Our histories will repeat unless we can identify the long-held beliefs that are still operating and leading us to the same results. It took me a long time in sobriety to even acknowledge that I had anger or even to feel angry. I was angry but didn't know it. When I did my first real fourth step in a twelve-step program, after numerous half-assed attempts, I was asked to list my resentments with people "with whom I was angry." I told my sponsor I wasn't angry and that I had already worked through all that stuff. Two hundred names and three hundred resentments later, I realized I was angry.

My anger showed up as a detached, smiley-faced, anxious, irritable, restless angst, mixed with over-functioning, isolation, and denial. Crazy making. I went from someone who didn't think she was angry to witnessing right in front of me hundreds of resentments on paper. Who was this person?! The thing is, I am a nice person. I'm kind, I'm funny, I'm a good friend, but I was also really pissed off. How did I not know? Anger can be disguised in many, many ways. One way I concealed anger was that I became a person who developed the adaptive behaviors of people-pleasing, conflict avoidance, and an inner denial of my true feelings. The problem was that by trying to control all these things, I would push my needs aside to please others, which was a recipe for repressed anger.

Sometimes we are so unconscious of our hidden or repressed anger that it manifests in a variety of ways. A few examples are:

- Lateness
- Speaking in a monotone voice
- Avoidant behaviors
- Overly accommodating, denial, flirtation
- Always being preoccupied
- Passivity, "forgetting," creating chaos
- Over-exercising or (over anything) restlessness
- Body pain, stomachaches (any kind of ache)
- Depression, anxiety (including panic attacks)
- Talking incessantly, being controlling
- Fatigue, trouble sleeping, sarcasm, criticism, and plenty more

Another example of getting activated often happens with our children. I remember when my son was a toddler and would take off on me in a clothing store and hide underneath a rack. I would completely panic and get so mad. The truth is, I was terrified that something would happen to him. The feelings were intense, and I didn't want to scream at him. I learned to begin to ask myself a couple of questions when I would feel intense anger, such as "What am I afraid of?" The typical answer was about not having control and feeling powerless, which was about earlier negative experiences. This level of rage had nothing to do with my son. It had everything to do with my past and my fear and powerlessness. It isn't that it's not scary to lose your toddler in a store, but the skill we need to learn over time is to not take out our intense fears and anger on others.

The key to resolving anger is to begin to look at how you relate to it. Do you deny it? Avoid it? Is it scary? Or are you completely unaware of your anger and maybe using other coping skills to mask it? One way to look at it is to see that each time you are angry, there is an underlying fear and hurt attached to it. What is being broken open right now? We may have had horrible things happen to us in the past, but it is our responsibility to not let that seep out onto everyone around us, especially our children. The important thing is to be able to identify feelings, experience them, express them, acknowledge them, and work through the anger.

The problem is that we continue to create problems in our relationships *and* carry these invisible resentments, while the focus of our resentments is *often out living their lives totally unaware of the turmoil we are experiencing.*

One therapist said to me, "When you say you feel crazy, you mean you're angry." True. Another therapist said, "You feel crazy when what you're really experiencing are intense bodily sensations that become overwhelming." Also true. I discovered that most of the time it was an old rage. I've even thought when I use the word "crazy" in regards to myself that I mean I'm feeling overwhelmed, misunderstood, not listened to, and confused. Sometimes we feel crazy in a relationship because we are enraged but repress our anger. Anger can be an identity, a way of functioning, a way to survive, a defense, a mask for hurt, pain, fear, powerlessness, or trauma. There are endless reasons for anger.

Fear and powerlessness. What was I feeling powerless over? There were numerous incidents from growing up and the addiction years where I felt trapped and not in control. This was the origin of my anger. What do you do when you feel powerless? If you ask yourself this question, you will be able to identify some of your go-to behaviors that you use to protect yourself. Humans hate powerlessness.

Once we identify these behaviors, we can then develop new ones that work more effectively in our close relationships. We can stop participating in behaviors that disguise our anger and perpetuate dysfunction. By taking responsibility, owning our behaviors and their consequences, embracing our pain and anger, and starting to dance with new possibilities, our new behaviors will lead us to more gratifying and fulfilling relationships. Trust that things will get better. Trust that there can be a new way. Trust that you don't have to be angry anymore to protect yourself. Trust that you will not lose your power by giving up your anger—you will get yourself back.

Tips for Working with Anger

- Give yourself a break. We can beat ourselves up over crap we have done out of anger—you can deal with that eventually. For now, this is just about assessing your relationship to anger.

- We all manage anger differently. The first step is working on becoming aware when you are having feelings of anger and not act out. Breathe. Walk away. Take ten. Pause. (God is in the pause.)

- Remember your anger is about you. You are the one carrying it. Nobody is doing it to you. Be brave. You can do this. Choose life rather than chronic anger.

- Some people can activate our anger like no other. Some people are what I call my "spiritual practice." Be grateful for them. They will help change you more than you can imagine.

- Start to get familiar with what is from the past and what is happening in the present. I did this by noticing that when I felt an intense activation in my chest, it was about the past. If I felt a mild irritation, agitation, or frustration, it may be about the present, but also related to the past.

Questions to Dive Deeper

1. What is your go-to anger response or behavior and how does this affect your relationships?

2. What do you use to avoid experiencing, expressing, or working through anger? Examples: addictions, manipulation, stay busy, shut down, people-please, act out.

3. What are the top five things you are angry about? What is the wound/sadness underneath the anger? What is the fear underneath the anger? What is getting in the way of resolving this, especially when we are not relying on other people to change?

4. What are the themes underneath the anger? Examples: I never feel heard, I'm always being taken advantage of, nobody loves me.

5. What stories do you make up about others and yourself when you get angry? Identify whether they are really true. Co-crazy is about blame. Recovery is about owning our part and realizing we can't control others. Give the other person to God.

Here's an example:

A client comes in who is having trouble in relationships. He seems to get activated a lot by his present wife when she asks him to do things around the house. He feels controlled, demeaned, and frustrated, and ends up lashing out at her. There could be numerous sources for this anger. He may have grown up in a household where his mother was controlling. His dad may have been an alcoholic. He witnessed over-the-top rage at small things, so he may be afraid of his own anger.

Every time his wife asks him to do something, he feels less than, not good enough, like a failure, and unloved. An old memory may even be triggered of being dumped by his high school girlfriend he was in love with. He believes he is unlovable and he lives with the fear that everyone will leave him. Neither of these things is true, but he lives with the chronic fear underneath the anger. When his wife asks him to do something, it triggers feelings of being less than and not respected. On and on it goes. Even fifty years later, buried anger can resurface.

The point here is that if we look deep enough, we can see that he had unresolved resentments from the past affecting his present relationships. He also was living out of old fears from past events that were keeping him in an endless cycle of fear and resentment. He was acting out earlier untrue beliefs that led him to behaviors that kept him stuck.

CO-CRAZY REMINDER

If there is an intense reaction, it is not about the present. It is already inside of you, and someone just activated that hurt.

12

Fear

I hadn't known I was angry, and I hadn't known I was run by fear. Lots of fear. But after doing step work in several programs and being in therapy for a zillion years, the final conclusion was: I'm terrified of everything. Feeling fear is part of being human, but like with anger, we try not to think about it. We may realize the big ones like fear of death or fear of getting sick or fear of losing a loved one, but I discovered that I was run by "a hundred forms of fear," as it says in the textbook of *Alcoholics Anonymous*. Most importantly, fear is the main operating system when it comes to co-crazy relationships and behaviors.

The unconsciousness of the fear and the automatic transition into a survival skill takes away our freedom of choice, but we don't even know it. We don't realize we are being run by our earliest fears rather than experiencing our true selves. The trouble comes when you are still using these survival skills at thirty, forty, fifty, sixty, and seventy years old. Most co-crazy humans live and die without recognizing that their entire lives were run by fear that directed their everyday behavior. We think we're in charge, but we're not.

When we are crippled by anxiety or have developed a personality to adapt to early fears, it is hard to get to know our true selves. My first way of coping with fear was overeating, and then

CO-CRAZY REMINDER

When we are unconscious of our fears, it comes at a high cost. The underlying fear driving us creates a distance between our authentic selves and who we really want to be in a relationship. The greater the distance between how we truly feel and how we act in our relationships, the higher the possibility for depression, anxiety, physical problems, and more. When we don't feel safe to be ourselves, we will have a greater need for distraction and escape, leading to addictive and co-crazy behaviors.

it became alcohol and drugs. None of these coping skills helped me to deal with fear—they just repressed it. I didn't even know what I was feeling, let alone that I was afraid. I knew I was anxious, but that's it. Recovery from co-crazy is about identifying those actions that helped you survive earlier but may not be helping now. Initially, you want to have compassion for yourself for creating some brilliant tactics to navigate your environment, but anything that stops you from revealing your true spirit isn't worth keeping.

It isn't like all these fears were *consciously* running my life. My behaviors were automatic actions that had developed over time to help me cope with unhealthy environments. We become as self-reliant as possible (or use other coping skills) to maneuver our way through relationships, experiences, and challenges to save us from our pain. How can we cope in our painful worlds of unpredictability, feelings of being out of control, or chronic anxiety without killing ourselves with some substance or acting out in some way that hurts us? This is the central conflict. We need to be brave enough to try new strategies and trust that we can still get our needs met without compromising ourselves or trying to control everything.

Some skills continue to work as we mature, and others get in our way of intimacy and being our true selves. For example, when I felt the fear of other people's opinions, I behaved in a particular way to avoid the fear.

These were some of my go-to survival skills: People-pleasing, isolation, repression, distraction, focusing on others, staying busy, perpetually smiling, being happy, avoiding feelings, lying, refusing to acknowledge reality, hiding out, acting out, eating, drinking, and flirting.

All of these behaviors were ways I tried to mitigate, control, or avoid a fear. My behaviors were there to protect and distract me, mainly to avoid underlying uncomfortable feelings. I didn't realize I wasn't choosing these ways of being. They had become automatic responses. Who was I underneath all of these defenses?

Before recovery from co-crazy, I didn't feel safe just being myself, so I spent most of the time managing the underlying fear by some personality adaptation. I began to get more and more detached from what I thought, how I felt, and what I wanted. My existence was about being validated by the outside world due to the paradigm that my self-esteem came from others. I wasn't hiding out with substances anymore, but now I was using old strategies to protect myself, and I was completely oblivious to these behaviors.

For example, if someone liked me or thought I was good at something, I felt okay. But if the outside world responded negatively to something I said or did, then I would not feel okay. How I felt about myself was entirely based on how the world interacted with me, not how I felt about the world. I couldn't know what my thoughts and feelings were because I was too busy worrying about everyone else's feelings and what they thought of me. Self-centered fear was running the show. This is a sure-fire recipe for inauthenticity, detachment from feelings, and not knowing what your own real thoughts are because you're imprisoned by other people's opinions. Zero freedom to be you.

When I began to realize how pervasive my fear was and how it directed my behaviors, I felt rattled to the bones. What was my true personality, besides fear and anger? I knew I presented as happy and outgoing. If you met me, you would have never

CO-CRAZY REMINDER

Don't rely on others to give you your value. It has to come from you and God. You are a precious being. Nobody gets to tell you who you are; only you do—so make it good.

thought I was afraid. We can all disguise ourselves pretty well, but even though I put up a good front, chronic anxiety was still always present. In recovery, I learned that many fears were controlling my life as a result of my history, but certain ones were the captain of the ship.

I discovered I had many different kinds of fear, from being afraid of different animals, bugs, and heights, to the interpersonal fears. These were the more important fears to recognize. These were the fears that came up when I was in relationships. These were the fears that blocked me from speaking my truth and being who I really wanted to be. There are only two fears that we are born with through evolution: the fear of falling and the fear of loud noises. All of the other fears you may have were developed due to certain circumstances where you experienced fear and then internalized it, linking it with a belief system and the creation of survival skills.

Some common fears with co-crazy: Fear of other people's opinions, fear of rejection, fear of not being liked, fear of not being loved, fear of not being good enough, fear of abandonment, fear of conflict, and the fear that something is wrong with you. The list is endless. We can connect most of the fears to particular incidents from our past. The key for me was discovering what beliefs I created from each incident that led to behaviors that were running my life.

The major fears operating in my life:

- Fear of no control
- Fear of not being wanted
- Fear of other people's anger

These are common fears and many people have them for a variety of reasons. Some are benign and some are traumatic. My main fear was the fear of no control. It came from growing up with a lot of unpredictability and years of addiction. The more traumatic the event that creates the fear, the more severe the behaviors become to avoid feeling out of control. To see where my fears originated, I went back through my life and got honest. Fears can arise with a particular incident and then be confirmed as we live out the belief system we created.

I'm sure many of you have had incidents where you were afraid. Start to break down what you decided about yourself, the world, and others after the experience. It's essential to process the event, but more important to realize how that event has now developed into ongoing behaviors and beliefs in which you create your life. This is what happened to me.

When I was seventeen years old, I had a terrifying experience that solidified my need to be in control. I include this because I believe many people who become addicts or who develop co-crazy behavior may have had similar incidents where they felt ashamed and terrified, leading to the development of a chronic anxiety or a need to seek approval from the outside world.

One night, I went to a bar in Boston with a friend of mine because I had a crush on the bartender. I dressed provocatively (fear of not being loved). My belief was, to get a man to want me, I needed to show off my body (distorted belief system). I was filled with the desperation of the eighteen-year-old who needed to be loved and seen. I met up with my friend Beth, and as the night wound down, she left. I was getting more and more drunk in hopes that Brad, the bartender, would want to be with me. My longing was real and palpable, yet my behavior to meet this need wasn't going to get someone to truly love me.

At the end of the night, Brad asked me to come to his apartment a few doors down. I remember thinking, *Oh my gosh, he likes me. I can't believe it.* I was very drunk, so some of this is foggy. Here's what I do remember.

I got there, and I was in a room, and suddenly, about five to six men circled me, and then I heard somebody say, "Which one of us are you going to do first?" I was simultaneously devastated and terrified. I screamed and said, "Let me out." I went running to a door that had a lock at the top. I remember struggling with that lock for what felt like hours but it was probably only forty seconds. I thought I was going to die. I remember standing at that door struggling to get it unlocked, trembling, drunk, and turning slightly to see if someone was going to stop me. They were all in a circle with beers in their hands and their heads back laughing with one another. I will never forget that scene. I escaped from that room and ran down the street to my car. My shirt was open—I don't remember why—but I was alive, shaken, and sobbing.

When I processed this event in therapy years later, I realized that many of my behaviors with men were about needing to escape. I frequently felt trapped. This feeling was inside my body. Nobody was doing this to me. It was a traumatic memory, now firmly established in my nervous system. Belief systems were then created about men, and these led me to future behavior without awareness. The traumatic experience cemented my already developed need to be in control. That incident happened during my senior year of high school and explained the escalation of my drinking and drug use during this time. This is just one of many incidents that created different fears that were running my life. In recovery, finally, the pieces began to come together.

I needed to learn to trust myself. I was in control of my body and I could now make decisions that were right for me. To change my behaviors from focusing on others to focusing on myself was the quintessential component in my recovery from co-crazy. I didn't want to be run by fear anymore. I needed to find my voice. I needed to speak my truth in relationships. I needed to give myself the gift and freedom of being my authentic self, no matter what others think. Period.

We are run by fear originated in an experience or event and we make up stories about what it means, then act on those beliefs. The fear of no control as a result of an incident would make my decisions about relationships, and I'd somehow create the delusion that I had control. It is ridiculous, but we all do it every day.

Due to continued investigation into my fear, I had the awareness that my fear of abandonment led me to two marriages. I loved both these men with all my heart but didn't recognize that fear was running the show. Our fears do not just affect us; they severely affect others. At thirty-nine years old, I was so afraid that I would never get married and never have a wedding that I married someone who wasn't the best match. I was unconscious of this motivation at the time. It is entirely unfair to make choices about other people's lives motivated by fear, but we do it all the time.

When I was dating my second husband, I told him immediately that I didn't want to get married. I loved being with him but I had no need to get married. I liked living alone. I had my son. I was fine just dating, and life was good. So why did I get married nine months later? I remember the day he proposed to me. He asked me to marry him by reaching into his pocket and putting a small box on the table in the Ninety Nine Restaurant. (This already pissed me off, I mean, the Ninety Nine Restaurant?) I thought to myself, *I don't want to get married. I told him I don't want to get married. We don't know each other well enough.* What came out of my mouth? "Yes." That decision was due to fear. Being driven by unconscious fears does not just lead to small consequences. Fear can lead us to making life-changing decisions. It happens all the time. Take a breath. No judgment. Just facts.

Tips for Working with Fear

- Start noticing when you are afraid and what situations may activate it. Realize that many of our fears are unconscious and running us all the time.

- Try to identify five of your fears that affect your communication and relationships, such as fear of conflict, fear of abandonment, fear of OPOs (other people's opinions), fear of rejection, fear of someone getting angry.

- Identify ways you mask your fear. Example: you act arrogant because you fear you aren't smart enough, or you agree too much due to the fear of upsetting others, or you stay quiet because you're afraid of what people will think if you speak up.

- Think of some new behaviors to use in these situations when you have a fear reaction.

Questions to Dive Deeper

1. Start looking at when the fear began. What happened? What feels familiar about this present fear? How long has it been there?

2. What are the belief systems created out of this fear that are no longer true? Create a new story.

3. How have you been living or not living because of this fear? Ex.: I avoid risk-taking because I'm afraid of failure.

4. What behaviors do you do to avoid fear or not feel it? Ex.: addictions, distraction, focusing on others, staying busy.

5. What are some new behaviors that could help ameliorate the fear?

Leaving Crazy Town

Get to Know Yourself

First, recognize that we are all the same. Nobody is better than or less than anyone. We are all experiencing this human condition as best we can. Whether it is therapy, a twelve-step group, a meditation retreat, or a Tony Robbins seminar, it does not matter what you do to get to know more about yourself. Just do something. If we are escaping through a substance or another person, we lose the connection to ourselves. When you know yourself, you can sit quieter, have more peace, and be more fully self-expressed. It is helpful to begin to be aware of what you react to, what your buttons are, and what you like and don't like. What are your interests? The possibilities for self-knowledge and awareness are limitless.

When I first got sober, I didn't even know what colors I liked or what style of clothing I wanted to wear. The leather halter top I had been wearing for years just didn't feel the same in sobriety. I loved Van Halen when I was drinking but couldn't listen to it when I got sober. I didn't know what I liked. I didn't know how to feel feelings. I began to realize I had choices.

Part of the problem—or the benefit—with focusing on someone else and being wrapped up in their drama is it fills our lives. It becomes a way to avoid taking responsibility for *our* daily fulfillment. It may be validating to have an identity we have created as caretakers, which may mean it is scary to look inside rather than outside for validation. It is okay to care for others, but this co-crazy type of caretaking kills people. It destroys their lives, their will, and their feelings of their own accomplishments. All because we think that *we* need to be responsible for *them*.

It is both a cosmic joke and a painful realization that it *not only* doesn't help the person in your life whom you are enabling but, simultaneously, you are sacrificing your own life and happiness to continue doing it. Even when it doesn't work. Addiction is a full-time job, and focusing on someone else's addiction or problems becomes a full-time job. What does it stop you from doing, or who does it stop you from being? What are you afraid of changing in your own life?

People can get comfortable with unhappiness. It's much easier to blame someone else for our frustrations and despair rather than to decide to create a life beyond co-crazy. I've seen numerous women and men who are in unhappy relationships begin to drink or use other distractions to cope. They don't know another way to deal with the problem, and subsequently, they are full of resentment. They feel underappreciated that they have sacrificed themselves for some greater good and nobody is acknowledging it. It won't get any better unless someone takes action. They want to change, they want a different life, but they are terrified of creating it. Change is scary, but life can be beautiful when we open our eyes, take responsibility, and open up to another possibility. A solution.

13

Co-Crazy Thinking: No Wonder I Felt Crazy

When we are in a relationship where we want someone to change, our thinking becomes distorted. On steroids.

We all have examples of this: thinking he is cheating when he is planning to propose, making up stories about what *they* are thinking, lying to ourselves to make their behaviors look reasonable, obsessions, and living in denial. The list is endless. Instead of being present in our daily life, we are stuck in our heads, spinning our agendas for the people around us. When we get sidetracked by our thinking, it's hard to know what is real and what is not. It is especially tricky in a relationship with an addict or alcoholic because they are likely lying to us. We jump on the rollercoaster of their insanity while trying to figure out our own reality.

The result is co-crazy thinking.

Distorted thinking is also part of the condition of mental illness, such as anxiety and depression. We can be so anxious that we think we are going to die, like experiencing a panic attack. We can even tell ourselves our lives aren't worth living, which can be part of depression. Distorted thoughts can go from mild, like making up a story that your sibling is mad at you because they haven't called in two days, to a complete psychotic break, such as with postpartum depression.

Most of us have distorted thoughts without knowing it due to beliefs developed during our early lives. An example would be that if my father abused me, I might have the belief that all men will hurt me. The co-crazy consequence is that we may then avoid men due to a fear of being hurt, or we might seek out men similar to our fathers to try to gain mastery over our past. Neither strategy works and as a result, we suffer.

We all see the world from a particular perspective. We forget that it is just a perspective, not necessarily reality. True freedom can only be experienced when we begin to create a friendly relationship with our thinking. It is important to become aware that our thoughts are just thoughts, but *we* attach the meanings. We don't have to allow ourselves to be overrun by thoughts or necessarily even believe them. We can just notice, create some spaciousness around them, and let them pass through.

One of the most important aspects of recovering from any-thing—substances, co-crazy, too much focus on that one thing, or a person you think is the answer—is to tell yourself the truth. The challenge here is that we may not know what's true. Or we may be in denial of the truth. Sometimes we know a particular truth but are terrified of acknowledging it. People think that if they become aware of something they are afraid of, they imme-diately need to take action. Not true. I knew I needed to quit smoking way before I did. My denial kept me smoking until my mother died of lung cancer. Reality has an interesting way of breaking up denial patterns.

It is often hard to see the truth about others. We lie to our-selves because we want a relationship to go a particular way, or we believe other peoples' lies because it is too painful to accept the facts. Just like with the example of my ex-husband Rob—it became very challenging to see the truth. He was telling me one thing, but I witnessed another. He would say he wasn't using drugs when his behavior made it evident that he *was* using, like nodding off during an important conversation. The statement

I hear most often is: "He/she is wonderful." This may be true, but their behavior may not be. The most important thing to do when we don't have clarity is to focus on our reality. What helps break through denial and give us clarity is what I call Sticking to the Facts.

Sticking to the Facts

This is one of the greatest tools to get clarity in any situation. We spend way too much time telling ourselves stories and making up scenarios. Focusing on facts is the primary tool used in interventions with substance abusers because they can't argue with facts. It is also a brilliant tool for anyone trying to get clarity in a problematic relationship or situation where we experience intense feeling states but either continue to repeat the same behavior or accept unacceptable behavior from others.

A girlfriend of mine recently expressed her frustration and pain over a decision to stay with her boyfriend. She loves this guy and feels like he could be the one. They have a lot in common, and well, he is super hot. So for about an hour, we sat at Starbucks, and she expressed her wishes, desires, fantasies, feelings, love, anger, and disappointment with this present relationship. She also struggled with questions like, "Is this person right for me? Does this guy love me? Will he stay committed to me?" (Notice all the questions are about what *he* thinks or feels rather than what *her experience* is.) We spent time breaking down what she liked about him and what she struggled with in the relationship.

Finally, I said to her, "What are the facts?" It took a while to get her to look at the facts, and even when she saw the facts, she still acknowledged to me that she wasn't ready to do anything. *Beautiful, honesty.*

- **Fact:** He is still married, although he hasn't lived with his wife for three years.
- **Fact:** He is not getting divorced.
- **Fact:** He lives three hours away.
- **Fact:** His son has a substance abuse problem, and he

is completely preoccupied and obsessed with his son's well-being.

- **Fact:** His wife is highly volatile and controls the family with her moods.
- **Fact:** He has major financial issues.
- **Bottom-line fact:** He cannot meet her needs and is unavailable.

This fact-based intervention may sound easy to most people, but have you ever tried to tell someone in love that you didn't think their beloved is the right person for them? The fact is that I don't know what's right for anyone else. However, we can work together to see what isn't working. I can have my opinions, but they don't help when it comes to matters of the heart. I can encourage someone to look at the facts, to help them with getting to a place of clarity, but telling someone what to do won't work. Stick to the facts.

It may seem like a simple problem to solve because he is married. Of course it won't work. But our minds tell us things will change, he will get divorced, he will get through all this unmanageability and one day "he will be who I want him to be." Maybe. What is painful is that she has fallen in love with this guy and now she may need to let him go. She may have to feel the loneliness, the disappointment, the grief, or the anger at herself for being in this situation. Sometimes we can know the facts but not be ready to face them.

The Both/And

My friend: "But he is really nice and has been sober for a long time."

Me: "I believe you."

During times of confusion we often want to make a firm decision. People get stuck in either/or thinking rather than acknowledging the both/and. People have numerous parts to them. We are complex beings and things aren't ever black or white, espe-

CO-CRAZY REMINDER

Always stay focused on the whole of what you are experiencing and feeling, rather than on what the other person is doing or saying. The bottom line is, it always comes down to what is best for us, not the other person. The co-crazy game is trying to control/change another while we continue to try to make their behavior okay so we will feel better. This leads to inaction. Come back to you, stay focused on your experience and what is happening inside you. Have I said this enough? It may be simple, but it's not easy.

cially in relationships. We often feel the need to gain some control, especially when there are intense feelings. We want to see our situation as all or nothing instead of embracing the whole of what is true. Many things in life are not all or nothing. They are complicated, full of gray areas, and uncertainty. It is crucial to be able to hold all of it to make a clear decision.

The facts in the previous example are that he *is* married, he *is* nice, he *is* preoccupied with his family situation, and he *is* hot. All of it. Otherwise, we get caught swinging on the pendulum between extremes, landing at one end on a particular day, and then when we get angry enough, we move to the other end. I have heard many clients come in one week ready to get a divorce, but then the next week, they are going away for a romantic weekend. There is nothing wrong with having challenges in a relationship and then making up. Still, if it becomes a *pattern* of behavior over time, we need to stay focused on what we want, not what the other person is doing or not doing.

The Intermittent Reward System: What Slot Machines Are Based On. Can Someone Say *Addiction*?

My marriage to Shane was full of ups and downs. One day, I would feel completely in love and that everything was okay, and the next minute I was thinking, *How did I get myself into this?* I craved consistency so I could experience some stability and hold on to the belief that this relationship would work. One minute we would have a deep connection. I felt loved and I enjoyed our life together. Then suddenly I would feel him pulling away. He would begin to say things like, "Maybe I made a mistake," "This may not be the relationship for me," or, "I feel ambivalent." Painful. But the minute *I* began to pull away, he would suddenly make some wonderful romantic gesture, and I would move back toward him. Things weren't bad all the time so I didn't want to end the relationship. I would take the bait and get back into believing that things would change.

It is at the moment when you get to the point of saying, "I'm done" that suddenly the dynamic shifts. They throw out a rope of hope, and we grab on. Just like walking away from the slot machine and then suddenly, you win a hundred bucks! What are you most likely to do? Stay at the slot machine and hope you win more money! This pattern is highly addictive and plays on our need for faith that things will change. Things may be bad for a while, and then we have a great connection with our sweetheart so we start thinking maybe it will work out. We start rationalizing, minimizing, and romanticizing—all the classic forms of denial—and then we have this occasional blissful evening, which leads us to continue to delude ourselves that things will be different in the future.

The randomness of the reward is what makes it addicting. It's not enough, and it's not consistent. You are stuck in an endless cycle of waiting for that great day once more. Just when you're ready to say, "F** k this," it magically occurs. There is an energetic dance of push/pull, avoid/attract, love/hate, good/bad, desperation/fulfillment, and pain/relief, which keeps us on the co-crazy train.

The commonly known pleasure/pain principle is similar to this, but it's not random. When something starts causing more pain than pleasure, we change it. Life, mental illness, and relationships aren't that simple, unfortunately. If they were, we would all leave unsatisfying relationships immediately, stop using drugs at the first consequence, or get help at the first sign of depression. Our distorted thinking keeps us in that magical cycle of believing things will change without taking action.

When we are in a relationship where we are ambivalent, but suddenly feel this deep connection during a beautiful time together, it is very easy to start thinking that things will be different, even though nothing has changed. The sudden hit of feeling loved or wanted can be so seductive and enjoyable that we may tell ourselves it is worth the wait.

Welcome to insanity.

The trouble is that the baseline gets lower and lower. It used to be great most of the time, then half the time. Now it's occasional, but we remember how great it felt when "we had that gorgeous weekend away in Maine" but it may have been six months ago. I have listened to men and women for years who have settled for very little to feel some kind of security. The irony is the security is an illusion and it could be gone in a split second. The real truth is that no matter how much you get, it will never be enough to fill that depletion or neglect from our past. It just continues to create more craving to fill it. It may help us cope temporarily, but the distorted thinking keeps us stuck in continuous dysfunction.

I have heard women gush about something their husbands did for them: they "babysat" their own child or cooked a meal, as if this was the second coming of Christ. I had a client who had a three-year-old and a one-year-old. When she arrived for her session, she was extremely anxious and admitted that it was the first time she had left her kids with her husband. The husband asked her on her way out, "What do I do if they get hungry?"

Feed them.

Some clients had tolerated such a low baseline for so long that when their partners did do something, they were overjoyed, forgetting that they hadn't done anything for years! This is not a judgment. It's a tragedy. Focusing on ourselves is critical. We need to develop the new reality that what we feel is important, and we deserve much more than what we have accepted. The harder truth is looking at what we have created as with the

CO-CRAZY REMINDER

It is easier to be clear about facts when you are upset. Just remember when you're feeling better, it doesn't mean the facts don't exist.

woman who was too fearful of giving up control to let her husband watch the children.

We tolerate certain behaviors because we are too afraid to give up control. Both people are responsible. We create these bargains with people, compromise ourselves, and then become enraged. We are part of the problem. Ouch again.

Tips for Working with Crazy Thinking

- List three facts of the co-crazy relationship you are in—good and bad, no judgment.
- Remember we are just looking at the facts. It does not mean you need to take action.
- Look at where you get into either/or thinking rather than both/and.

Questions to Dive Deeper

1. What are the parts of the relationship that would be hard to let go of?
2. Are you addicted to the drama in the relationship and avoiding what you really want?
3. Why is the chaos so seductive?
4. If you give percentages of time to when you're happy and fulfilled and when you're not, what would they be? Honesty is the key.
5. What are you willing to change?

14

Living on the Planet of Denial

There are many ways of thinking that we utilize to distract, avoid, and deny our crazy and co-crazy behaviors, thoughts, and feelings. These also help us to stay detached from ourselves and our experience and can lead us to focus on another and their problems. These are all ways we avoid our present reality and distance ourselves from the truth.

Rationalization

Rationalization is a common mode of coping and a form of denial. We can participate in a particular behavior then rationalize why we did it. When I was using drugs and alcohol, there were plenty of reasons I had to drink—my parents, my boss, my anger, "that guy," and my anxiety. I mean, if you had my life you would drink too, right? All rationalizations. Human Beings can rationalize *anything*. We use these beliefs to avoid the consequences of our behavior, to make ourselves look good, and to live in a fantasy world.

Rationalization is a way to avoid the truth and defend our behaviors. We see ourselves in a particular way, so if our behaviors don't match up with that belief system, we have to rationalize the behavior. Over the years, I have had people in my office rationalize lots of behaviors. Here is a partial list: affairs, addictions, relapsing, abusing someone, screaming at someone, hitting someone, marrying the wrong person, quitting a job abruptly, criticizing a child, not communicating something important, not setting limits, forcing kids to live out the parent's dreams, lying, and not calling that person back. They range from small stuff to big stuff.

Rationalization eats away at our soul. It's a way we stay in delusion and lie to ourselves. On a deeper level, we know what the profound truth is, but we also know we aren't ready to face it. It is hard for us to acknowledge the reality of our situation, but it feels impossible to do something about it. If there is something you have done and rationalized or blamed someone else for, and you feel this niggling at the back of your mind and it won't leave you alone, it will come out somewhere. You may start to act out, you may start using some substance, you may need to be on your phone all day, you may have an affair, or you may even work more. Whatever it is, it becomes too difficult to repress. Underneath all the busyness, the focus on others, and the preoccupations, is someone who knows the truth.

When my son was a couple of years old, I was exhausted and lonely. I met a wonderful man at a coffee shop. He was smart, talented, funny, and kind. He was also married. I could say that I didn't know. I could say that it was weird that I could only call him at work. The fact was that I did not want to know until I did. It took two months, and I rationalized it all. I would tell myself that he and his wife didn't have a real relationship. He was getting a divorce. Who were we really hurting if nobody knew? I deserved to get a break and have someone take me out. All bullshit. I wanted what I wanted. What I really wanted was relief. Relief from my feelings, relief from my pain, relief from my struggle and relief from my loneliness. All of it.

CO-CRAZY REMINDER

You can't live wrong and feel right.

Minimizing

Minimizing is another form of denial. We all have a hell of a time getting real. People who have substance abuse problems often minimize, but so do other people without addiction issues. Minimization is another way of thinking to avoid reality.

These are familiar minimizations that I hear in my practice: "He/she isn't that bad." "I only drank on Wednesday and Friday." "I only have two drinks a night." (The glasses were 16 oz. goblets with four shots in the drink.) "She only flirts with other guys when she drinks." My personal favorite is, "I only drink wine." I had a client once tell me he had been sober for three months. Then, in a later session, he told me he had drunk wine at a wedding.

I said, "Oh, I thought you were sober."

He replied, "Wine and beer aren't alcohol."

Gotta love it. Those alcoholic minds are lying to us endlessly, but we still want to believe everything they tell us.

We can minimize anything. I've heard couples who fight a lot say, "I know my kids aren't affected." Are you kidding? I was four years old and knew what was going on with my parents. Again, it is too painful for people to acknowledge how much their behavior is affecting others. Examples of minimizing: "I don't need to tell my husband/wife how I feel." "I'm not that depressed." "I'm only on six medications." "I'm not working too much; everyone at my office works sixty-five hours." "He only hit me twice." "She doesn't yell all the time."

It's a way to see things in a better light so we can feel okay about it. Our minds are highly skilled at trying to create equilibrium in our systems. I had a patient in a detox tell me he had "only been to detox sixty times" and he "knew a guy who had been a hundred times." Who knows if this was true but . . . is sixty detoxes a good thing? Minimizing can be a killer.

Do you realize how many mothers are guzzling wine starting at three in the afternoon and don't want to believe it is that bad? I'm not saying every mom who drinks wine is an alcoholic, but many of my clients who are moms began drinking heavily to deal with the enormous stress of having young children. The thought of quitting anything is too scary. When I was getting ready to quit, I decided to stop using cocaine but kept drinking. I just drank more. Brilliant.

I feel sick to my stomach sometimes when facing the truth about the times I have rationalized and minimized. When my husband Rob relapsed, I didn't want to face reality. I didn't want to believe that he couldn't get sober. I didn't want to look at how unmanageable our lives had become, and I didn't want to see what it could be doing to my boy.

The most painful thing for any mother to do is to look at the fears that keep us stuck and see how our behaviors have affected our children. I was living in a survival mode. I believe I was doing the best I could, but I also know that my denial went on longer than I wanted to admit. When Rob forgot to pick up my son at school one day, and Max wasn't at home when I returned from work, I couldn't deny the facts anymore.

My addict husband was now impacting my son. I had to do something. I'm not a hero because I left. I stayed until I couldn't avoid the pain of reality. Coming out of denial can be heart-breaking.

Romanticizing

Romanticizing is the way our mind tricks us into believing that our perceptions of reality are much rosier than the truth. I've had clients who are still talking about their wild adventure at Woodstock. They quit drinking thirty years before but were blocking out where drinking took them in the end. I've had clients who have been married for thirty-five years, still talking about the first ten and believing that someday, even though they are miserable, they will magically return to that great feeling.

It's focusing on an aspect of our lives in a way that makes it seem lovely and beautiful without acknowledging the painful parts to see the full picture. It is a form of denial that keeps people stuck. I once had a woman write on a calendar when her boyfriend was abusive to her. She kept talking about the first couple of years of their relationship as if it was still fulfilling. Her boyfriend had verbally abused and controlled her for the previous five years, but her perception was that it only happened occasionally.

When we reviewed the facts of the frequency of arguments, it was revealed that she was screamed at and criticized regularly. She struggled with letting go of the fantasy of her relationship. She used minimizing and romanticizing to stay stuck and to keep her from facing her fears of leaving.

Looking at the facts can break through denial but often will lead to a bigger issue. Do you want to do anything about it? This is the underlying fear of why people stay in denial. We don't want to face the truth because the option of taking action seems more painful. It requires energy to take action. It is more of an emotional than a physical effort. We need to be able to tolerate feelings of the unknown, change, regret, loss, fear, anger, and grief. We need to trust that we are heading toward something better.

Some people never get clarity because there is so much fear operating, and they become paralyzed. This is a personal decision that we only make when somebody crosses the line, and then we get the clarity we hadn't seen. That line is different for everyone.

Intellectualizing

During my years in practice, the most challenging clients were the ones who thought their intellect was going to help them solve their addiction problem. I call it "the wall of words." Just stop already. Addiction isn't something to figure out with your mind because the quintessential component of addiction is denial which is a cognitive process. So, all our minds are going to tell us are lies or rationalizations. This makes it impossible to see the truth. Interventions work because people just talk about the facts of how they were affected by the addict. In my practice, the more attached someone was to their intellectual abilities as a defense against feelings, the truth, and reality, the tougher it was to help them.

People have used their intelligence to thrive, accomplish, and have great successes in particular areas of their lives, so it is hard to surrender to the fact that your thinking won't help you with addiction. The smarter people were, the more likely they would try to convince me that they were right, didn't need help, could figure it out, or had all the answers. They were in just as much pain as any of my less-intellectual clients but found it much more challenging to acknowledge that pain. The defenses were up, and the denial was active. I've asked several patients at the psych hospital where I worked to "check their address" when they wanted to debate me about how they weren't "that bad."

Fact: You are in a psych hospital for alcoholism.

We cannot help people who aren't ready to hear what we have to say. It is odd at times because someone may be struggling with a relationship or depression or addiction and ask me for help. I give them my best stuff—brilliant tools that have worked forever—and they say, "Okay, thanks, but I think I'll do it my way" even though it is clear that their way is *not* working. It's someone's right to take action or not take action, but it mystifies me if I have just told you what works for many, many people, why would you want to waste any more time figuring it out? Ego perhaps; fears mostly. Fear mainly of doing something that *they* didn't think of and not knowing if it will work. What then? It is also about trust. A person who needs help has to trust someone and be willing to try something new. They also may have to be in enough pain to motivate them to change.

Do you know how many people I have had in my office who thought they should rewrite the main textbook of 12-step recovery titled *Alcoholics Anonymous*? Lots. Do it. Great. Contribute, but maybe it is time to listen. If you are in a therapist's office, a psych hospital, or your life is falling apart, maybe it's time to notice how you got there.

A sober friend of mine is a real intellectual. He is a lovely person and extremely smart. He wants to discuss jazz music or certain types of art or particular spiritual practices. At times when I'm with him, my eyes begin to narrow, I get a skeptical

look on my face and think, *What the f**k is he talking about?*
The problem is, he keeps looking for more and more ways to
move away from himself. His life is a relentless, restless effort
to manage the outside world so he doesn't feel afraid, but he's
oblivious to what motivates his behavior.

He is constantly talking about the next thing he is going to
buy, or the next place he is going to visit, or the next musician he
needs to listen to. Underneath all that intellect is just a scared
boy who was brutally beaten by his dad. Being smart doesn't help
him heal, but it does help him to temporarily feel "better than"
so he doesn't have to feel the deep past insecurities of being poor,
feeling less than, and like he didn't belong. He is operating as if
he still needs to prove something to the world, when he needs to
grieve the relationship with his dad so he can be himself rather
than this super intellectual know-it-all who keeps himself safe by
staying distant from others. Learning how to identify what fears
are underneath the intellectualizing would be the beginning of
his healing journey.

Why is everyone attached to being right? Especially when
they are suffering and trying to get help. Who cares what the
answer is as long as it is helpful? You don't need to agree with it;
you just need to start doing something different. We are trying to
solve a problem of our minds (addiction) with our minds. Doesn't
work. It's like asking a person in a manic episode if they want to
take their medication. Of course not.

Our minds are not going to give us the right answer unless
we get off the drugs and alcohol or get help with our co-crazy
behaviors. We have this need sometimes to be precious or different because we've never felt loved. It's the belief that "I know
it works with most people but not me. I'll show them." We want
to be unique and smarter than the outlier—even when it is
killing us.

Tips for Working with Denial

- Get some support. Whether it is a support group, indi-
  vidual therapy, a good friend, or an online community.

Changing behaviors is challenging—don't do it alone. Remember, you have used these defenses for a reason.

- Be gentle with yourself if you're not ready. This is not about beating yourself up. Beginning to acknowledge your truth can be heartbreaking, but it's about finding freedom with yourself and in your relationships to be who you want to be.

Questions to Dive Deeper

1. What behaviors are you presently participating in where your rationalizing, minimizing, romanticizing is driving you?

2. What are the *facts* of your own behaviors behind these defenses of denial?

3. What do you believe you will "figure out on your own" that you may need help with?

4. What is the hard truth that is difficult to face?

Some examples of addressing these types of thinking are:

- I have minimized my own drinking over the years. The fact is I drink six drinks a night.

- I have rationalized how much I scream at my kids. The fact is I'm always angry and taking out my anger on them.

- My spouse works hard to support the family (rationalization, minimization, or only part of the picture of the relationship). Fact: he is never home, and we don't have a connection. Also true.

- I want to be in the truth about my marriage, so I realize I've been rationalizing how angry my husband is. I will stick to the facts, write down my truth, find some support, and think about ways I can behave around this new reality. I can focus on speaking my truth. I can talk to him about couple's therapy. I can start focusing on my own life and behavior rather than on what he is doing or not doing. I can look at my options and create new ones. You only have the power to change yourself, not him.

15

Living in Fantasyland

One of the problems with being a human being is that we tend to believe our thoughts. The most important part of healing from co-crazy is to begin to create a loving and spacious relationship to your thinking. Our minds can make up stuff all day long, we believe it and then act on it. This is another form of insanity. Our minds are thought-producing machines. That's what they do. Our job is to begin to just notice them as possibly interesting—maybe entertaining—but definitely not always true. Just begin to notice. This is how we slowly step out of fantasyland.

Making up Stories

Making up stories is a major part of the human condition. I don't mean creative stories like a novelist but making shit up in your head all day long about what others think, who others are, what they are like, what they do, whether they are good people or bad, or forming judgments. This practice is bad enough, but then we act out and respond to our made-up fiction. We make up a story, tell ourselves a lie, and then act on it. In the textbook of *Alcoholics Anonymous*, there is a sentence describing this way of thinking.

> *"Driven by a hundred forms of fear, self-delusion, self-seeking, and self-pity, we step on the toes of our fellows, and they retaliate..."*
> —Alcoholics Anonymous

It is brilliant. This sentence describes the thinking of an alcoholic but also the thinking of most human beings when fear arises. It describes the behaviors we act out when we become afraid and the inevitable consequences. The trajectory goes from fear to self-delusion to self-seeking to self-pity. Here's an example. Let's start with a common one, the fear of other people's opinions. I'm walking down the hall at work. I pass my boss who is preoccupied with looking through a file as she is walking by me. I say, "Good morning." She doesn't say anything back to me. As a response to this, I begin to make up the story in my head that she doesn't like me. What have I done wrong? I must have done something. Did she not like the work I've done on the project so far? I bet that's it. Maybe she doesn't like the way I wrote it. Should I write it over? Did she even talk to me at the Christmas party? Did I say something offensive? My head is spinning.

Fact: I said good morning to my boss, she may not have heard me, and she didn't say anything back.

We have a fear and then we start lying to ourselves. This is called self-delusion. We start making up all kinds of stories based on our past histories. We don't think to ourselves, *Oh, maybe my boss didn't hear me,* or *Gee, she must be busy with work.* Some people may not take it personally and see reality, but most of us who have a history that created co-crazy begin to fabricate a story in our heads because we are so preoccupied with others' thoughts and feelings. We make up that what she did or didn't do has something to do with *us*—self-centered fear. Then the self-seeking behaviors kick in. How do I now change this? How do I figure out a way to get my boss to like me again? Reminder: Nothing has happened.

I decide to re-work my project and change some writing that I *imagine* she may not like. Notice the word *imagine*. I also decide that maybe I should have bought her a Christmas gift. We don't usually do that, but I conclude from made up thinking that I missed a memo. I buy her a lovely flower vase on my lunch break and have it wrapped. This is the self-seeking behavior to get my boss to like me because I had decided she didn't like me based on one interaction. All fantasy. I call her and set up a meeting for four o'clock. I walk in with a gift in hand and my project with all kinds of changes. She looks perplexed. I realize that none of the stuff I made up was true. Now I look like an idiot and wonder how to explain the gift. When I leave her office, I wallow in self-pity, all because of a situation I created! Sound familiar? That is one example of what we do *all day long.*

A friend of mine would frequently give the example of walking down a street and seeing a couple and deciding right away that he hated them because they were obviously rich and happy. This constant projecting and inner storytelling is a crazy way to live. It is living in a fantasyland, but humans do it all the time. To get peace, you have to create a loving relationship with your mind and embrace the craziness, notice it, and acknowledge it, but not act on it. Remember, thoughts are just thoughts. They are not necessarily true.

Mind Reading

I learned this lesson over and over when my son was a teenager. When he came home from school he wouldn't say much. I would suddenly be off and running in my head thinking something must have happened to him at school. Did someone bully

CO-CRAZY REMINDER

No matter how much you believe that you can tell who people are by just looking at them, or you believe you know what they are thinking, you can't. Seriously, you can't. No, seriously.

him, did a girl hurt him, did a teacher shame him, did he fail a test...? Notice I'm not saying it's anything he'd done. I decided there must be something seriously wrong, so I'd bug him about it.

Me: "Bud, what's up?"
Max: "Nothing."
Me: "Really, you sure? You seem quiet."
Max: "Yeah, Mom, I'm quiet. I've been in school all day, just want to chill."

This co-crazy dialog would go on and on until he wanted to kill me, and I was in tears. I would make up some story that my son wasn't okay due to my own fear. He was fine. I was the one who wasn't okay. Bad idea to get into the pattern of getting into people's business and making up a story that something is wrong with them when there isn't! People can communicate what they need, or if they can't, let them learn. My son was telling me he was fine. I have learned that you say it once and let it go.

Me: "Max, do you think you need your coat today?"
Max: "No, Mom, I'm all set."

He is now nineteen years old. Do you think he knows whether he is cold or not? I'm worried he will be cold but he isn't. So whose issue is it?

Obsessive Thinking: When the Crazy's Got Us

The addict is obsessed with finding their drug, and their partner is obsessed with trying to control their behaviors. The core to

CO-CRAZY REMINDER

Leave people alone when they tell you to. When people answer your question, believe them. Don't keep bugging them because you want to alleviate your own anxiety. Look inward, not outward.

obsessive thinking is fear. When fear gets activated in our systems, our brains become hyper-focused on something outside of ourselves to ameliorate it. It is not only obsessive thinking with addiction. We can also begin to think that if only we can fix, change, control, get that thing or person, we will be okay, we will *feel* okay, but it is a temporary fix to a bigger problem. Sitting with what we are experiencing without doing anything is hard to do when the feelings of fear—or anything else—can be so intense, distressing, and unbearable.

Obsessive thinking is the part of addiction where we become obsessed with a specific substance then take the action of searching for it, finding it, and using it. The behavior is supposed to stop the obsession but instead creates the cycle of addiction where once we finish the substance, we want it again. Often the trouble with "controlled drinking" or controlled anything is that the behavior may stop intermittently, but the obsessional thinking gets worse. Just because we decide only to take a drink on Monday, Wednesday, and Friday does not mean we aren't going to now *think* about it all the time. The compulsion is now being somewhat controlled but this won't last long because the obsession increases.

When obsessive thinking gets activated, it isn't just that we begin to experience the underlying fear. There is also an activation of the fight/flight/freeze response to old buried trauma. This may not always be the case, but I have sat with clients who cannot let go of an obsession because they feel like they will die. An old primal wound inside them unravels, and their coping skills become the obsession. It is not easy, but it's critical to figure out what healthy coping skills you can use so you don't get driven by an obsession. Creating strategies like finding a distraction, physical activity, or writing—anything to break that inner loop of thoughts—is helpful. If it isn't getting better, get help from others to support you to understand what is underneath this thinking.

My friend Kelly called me this morning and began talking about her boyfriend, Ralph. She had spoken to him the previous night, and he had a high temperature. In the morning, he told her he would go to urgent care. However, he hadn't called by eleven, and now she was out of her mind. The obsessive thinking had taken over and Kelly became consumed with his whereabouts: Was he dead on the side of the road? Had he run off with another woman? Was he unconscious in his car somewhere?

The answer? None of the above. The truth is, Ralph went to urgent care. He went back home and fell asleep. The doc diagnosed him with strep throat.

Her obsession was activated because of the fear of losing him. What intensified it and felt unbearable to her was the connection to an earlier experience of losing her dad. It's a small example where we often aren't even aware that a more significant issue is being activated. We just know it feels like life or death. We have a fear, it activates a behavior, and we find out it wasn't real. Or maybe it was, but the obsessive thinking doesn't help the obsessing person, and it did not control the outcome.

When I am triggered into some obsessive thought pattern, I ask myself, *What am I afraid of?* For example, I may be worried a friend is angry with me for something I said to her. I stay up all night ruminating and obsessing, and I can't let it go. I'm afraid of losing the relationship, and underneath that is the old *real fear* of losing my father's love. It isn't about my friend at all.

After an interaction, I can be vulnerable to making up stories that people are mad at me due to this early distorted perception that my father was *always* mad at me. I grew up in constant fear that my father was upset with me, and I was losing his love. In friendships or intimate relationships, I have to watch for this belief getting in the way of intimacy.

CO-CRAZY REMINDER

Obsessive thinking is a way to feel in control of a situation where we feel out of control. It is a way not to feel what is going on in our bodies, hearts, and minds, and focus on something else.

This underlying fear relentlessly gets acted out in relationships. One of the things I can do is a reality check. I can call and ask the person if they are upset with me. Most of the time, it is my fearful thinking, but if it is true, we can talk about it. In this situation, I'm not responsible for my friend's anger. I'm only responsible for my response. My obsessive thinking becomes a way that I can be hyper-focused and distracted in my mind rather than be present with the underlying feelings of grief, sadness, old terror, and loss. It takes practice and time to work through. When fear starts percolating, depending on the intensity, remember it is usually not about the present moment.

Defenses: Oh, Boy

My mantra after years of being in twelve-step programs is: there is nothing to defend (meaning when it comes to your ego). I repeat: Whatever comes out of somebody else's mouth is about them.

An important skill to learn is to listen, empathize, and validate when someone is speaking and not take everything they are saying as personal. Try to remember that they are sharing *their* experience. I do not have to immediately defend a position when they aren't talking about me. I may still have feelings come up inside, or a reaction, but I don't need to immediately speak up or overreact to my internal states. Stay present in the conversation and connection. Remember, if I have an intense response, it is usually about the past getting activated in the present. Whatever they are communicating is their issue, their thoughts, feelings, and opinions. It has nothing to do with me. I

CO-CRAZY REMINDER

The mantra, "I am not responsible for anyone else's thoughts, feelings, or behaviors" is tattooed on my brain. I am only responsible for my actions, my words, and my feelings.

can still feel my own feelings, respond appropriately, or express what is coming up for me. It can be a full-time practice at first to work through our unconscious activations, but it makes life much more comfortable in the long run because we don't end up being just a reaction machine. If we can own our reactions, we will have more harmonious and fulfilling relationships. We can't truly listen and have deeper connections when we are stuck in past anger affecting our day-to-day communications.

***

My son and I both love movies. We have had a ritual for years of going to the movies on Friday nights. As my son got older, it became more about him and his friends going to the film, and I would sit in another part of the theater. Then they were old enough to go to R-rated movies with a parent, and they loved horror movies. Meanwhile, I'm still traumatized from hiding under my seat when I saw *Day of the Dead* in the '80s. Many Friday nights I would be sitting on the other side of the theater, terrified with my hands in front of my face, trying to block the screen. I hit my limit while watching a movie called *It Comes at Night*. The boys loved it; I was psychically tortured for weeks.

The conflict came to a head one Friday night when a new horror film was released. Little did I know that he and his friends had made a plan to go to this new movie and I was supposed to be the chaperone. This meant more torture for me sitting in the movie because the boys weren't seventeen. I had already told Max that I couldn't watch horror movies anymore but I would see anything else. It came to a head at the ticket counter on a Friday night with seven sixteen-year-olds huddled around me.

Max begins the debate: "Mom, you said you would go in."

Me: "No, Max, I did not say that, I'm not going in. Pick another movie." *Stick to the facts.*

Max escalating: "But, Mom, we really want to go to this new movie. It's sooo good and you promised!" *No, I never promised but kids are brilliant.*

Me: "Max, pick another movie."

My brother the attorney always told me when you are in a debate, just keep repeating the same sentence and then shut up.

The crowd began lining up behind me and the tension was building. Oh, God. Suddenly, Max just lost it. He started walking away from me with his tribe following him and then he got to the door of the movie theater, turned around, looked right at me, and said in this evil, deep voice and drawn-out scream, "Mom, I HATE YOU! I haaaattttttteeeeeeee you!" Did I mention there was a long line of people?

OUCH. F**k. That was painful. Remember, pause when agitated or doubtful *or in incredible pain!* All his friends followed him outside. I did not say a word. What I wanted to say was, "How could you say this to me? I have brought you to the f***ing movies for the last ten years of my life *every* Friday! Are you serious right now? What the f**k? Do you know how much I've done for you? Really? Are you f***ing kidding me right now!?" But I knew at that moment it wasn't about me. What was coming out of my son's mouth was absolutely not about me.

What had happened was that he was embarrassed and ashamed that he had told all his friends that I was going to the horror movie, but his plan didn't work out. I let them figure it out, and eventually they went to another movie. The next morning, we talked, and he apologized for his behavior.

If I had gotten into it with him at that moment and tried to defend my position, it would have been a nightmare. Ninety percent of the things teens say to us are opportunities to react. If we can pause and breathe, it will save us a lot of heartache. The thing to remember is that when big emotions are happening, nothing will be resolved at that moment. If I can just sit with my feelings, notice, and trust that we can work it out another time, there is an opportunity for healing my own anger, fear, and co-crazy. Practicing this pausing consistently made me into a person my son could trust.

Taking responsibility for your own part, without defending, is a critical tool in harmonious relationships. Children will endlessly activate our issues. Parenting is the most significant opportunity to discover our pain and resolve it. Welcome to growing up.

No Judging, and It Isn't Personal

Most of what comes into our heads when it comes to making up stories is a result of all our experiences up until that moment. Our upbringing, our hurts, and our relationships are all still invisibly impacting us. It is hard to see with any clarity when we have a lifetime of experiences behind us. The beliefs and experiences from our past create all the thousands of judgments that cross our minds every day. Freedom comes when we don't get too attached to our judgments. The more I have done this pausing, the quicker the judgments leave my mind, and the less appealing they seem. Again, thoughts are just thoughts. Judgments are just thoughts. They come in, and they go out.

How many times have we had an experience that we think someone is a certain way and then they turn out to be completely different? All the time. I will be in a twelve-step meeting and I make up something in my head based on how a woman looks and my mind says, *Oh, she must not be friendly.* Or, *She doesn't know what she is talking about.* Then she opens her mouth and blows my mind with some profound and helpful insight. I have learned over the years to notice judgments, but they aren't worth giving any weight. Judging others is just a way to stay separate and feel safe.

This judging is not the helpful kind of judgment or discernment I'm referring to. For instance, "Should I date this person if he doesn't have a car or a job?" What I'm referring to is *being* judgmental. Most of us move through our day and have judgments or opinions pop up in our heads about a particular person's look, or attitude, or behavior, or vehicle, or food they eat, or *anything.* Other people's choices are none of our business. If what others are doing or saying affects our lives, then yes, we can speak up or take action. How we *respond* is our business but other people's choices are their business. We may have feelings about their choices, but that's it. Period.

We find it difficult not to interpret everything coming into our Hula-Hoop as personal. We forget people are on their own trip. Humans can be so driven by fear and self-centeredness that we can walk into a room and think everyone is talking about us. It is just more of making up stories and self-centered fear. The more afraid we are, the more we make stuff up. When we are trapped in our minds, our fears, our pasts, our hurts, and our deeply held resentments, we often forget that the outside world is moving right along without us. Moreover, we forget that every human being we come in contact with has their own perception of reality, their own truth, their own history, and their own beliefs. It is miraculous that any of us can even communicate with each other. We are carrying around every event, belief, hurt, trauma, and joy like a kid dragging their blankie, but we expect people to respond to us the way *we* would.

I have had many clients who struggle with going to recovery groups due to different fears. A client will walk into a room and think, *Everyone is staring at me*. Well, you walked into a room, and the door slammed, so people turned their heads. Again, self-centered fear is where we think everything is about us. An extreme case can border on paranoia, where you believe that someone in the room is talking about you. At the other extreme is someone who is unaware of their surroundings and is extremely internally focused.

Over time in recovery from co-crazy thinking, we can see how our fears can interpret our surroundings based on earlier established beliefs. We invent stories and end up stuck in the past. Going to a group or a meeting can activate old feelings. It is an excellent example of how self-centered fear can dominate our thinking. Groups may not be for everyone, but it is helpful to know what is operating so you're not unnecessarily blocked from getting well.

When clients attend a twelve-step group, here are some of the common complaints I hear when they return:

- People didn't like me. *This is based on someone looking at them a particular way.*

- Nobody talked to me. *Could it have been that you sat in the corner with your arms crossed with an angry look on your face?*

- I think a group of women was laughing at me. *They were laughing, but at you?*

- Nobody gave me their phone numbers. *Did you ask anyone?*

- I can't relate to anyone. *Okay, but you may want to think about identifying, not comparing.*

- They all seem to have problems. *Are you not in a twelve-step meeting?*

Fear causes us to perceive the world in a certain way that doesn't help us grow. Most people are thinking about themselves, and appropriately so. Unless you have some co-crazy. Then you may be instantly attracted to and begin falling in love with the craziest one in the room. I'm not saying twelve-step meetings are for everyone, but take a look at what your mind tells you when you get scared. (Remember: it lies.)

Another example of taking it personally is when a couple comes to therapy. One partner says, "He doesn't love me because he keeps drinking." The spouse is deeply wounded. Understandable, but not personal. Someone's addiction has nothing to do with whether they love you or not. It is hard to accept because living with an addict or alcoholic hurts like hell. It only means that the person we are living with is sick. We can do something about it rather than continuing to take it personally. This idea of separating the person from the addictive behavior is one of the biggest challenges for people living with addiction. I'm not saying it doesn't bring up tons of feelings, but try to think about them as someone with an illness.

When Shane and I moved to Boston from San Diego, he went through a severe depression. I remember thinking, *Come on, we just moved here. Great things are happening. We have a great place to live. Snap out of it.*

I was so understanding.

The fact is I did not want Shane to be depressed. I kept thinking, *This man is trying to ruin my life.* Nope, he was in enough pain without having to focus on my disappointment. First we try to have compassion and understanding, but if a relationship isn't working for you, take some action. It's never about sticking it out in dysfunctional relationships and continuing to be miserable. It is about understanding that other people's issues or behaviors are not about you. I remember hearing at a seminar years ago, "You can either interpret an event in a way to empower you or disempower you—you choose." It is difficult when we have automatic interpretations of what is happening in our environment. We need the spaciousness to get some detachment from our automatic thoughts so that we aren't believing every little thought alarm that goes off in our brains.

I often listen to the experiences of friends in relationships (which are commonly known as the *petri dish of our dysfunction*). They make up generalizations about men or women based on their pasts. "There are no good men out there." *I've met plenty.* Or, "Women just want a guy to support them." *Maybe some women.* These beliefs are limiting, and it may be a decision made after one bad experience. I've also had the experience of being at a party where a friend will say while noticing an attractive woman across the room, "Oh, she doesn't like me." I think, *You don't even know her. Talk to her.* People are thinking about themselves at a party, not you.

I used to be so consumed by fear and made-up thoughts in my head that I thought people around me were thinking about me until I realized one day that they are in their own world, thinking about themselves. Again, appropriately so! Our minds can tell us negative stories of what we believe people are thinking about us. What people think of me is none of my business. I know this is tough to comprehend. The only way we know what someone is thinking is if we ask them. That's it. Even then, we may not know if they are telling the truth. Oh well.

I don't care. I don't know. I'm confused.

(Otherwise known as, Yes, you do. Yes, you do. No, you're not.)

These things are what people say when they don't want to face something. Often, it's not wanting to confront an underlying fear. *I don't care* is a way we minimize our thoughts and feelings about something. Maybe we *sometimes* really don't care. It is one thing if we are asked, "Do you want Ethiopian coffee or Arabic?" But if your husband asks, "Do you really like this house? I just put an offer in on it," you may have some feelings about that. Saying, "I don't care" is a way we dismiss ourselves as if we don't have an opinion. We are afraid to express our real thoughts and views for a variety of reasons. It could be that we fear conflict, don't want someone to be mad, want someone to like us, or fear what it means if we disagree.

Saying "I don't know" is also a way to stay distant from yourself. There may be some information that you just don't want to acknowledge. Most people come to therapy because of relationship conflicts. When asked direct questions about the relationship, they may say, "I don't know." They obviously *do* have lots of thoughts and feelings about the relationship or they wouldn't be in my office, but people are afraid if we begin to discuss it, we may reveal a truth they don't want to know yet. I try to get a client like this to see that they are still in charge. The fear of speaking up or taking a stand about something may be hard with someone we love. It is a huge step forward in recovery to begin to speak up and say what is on your mind. You will begin to know that your thoughts and feelings are valid and essential.

I'm confused is a way to keep us from taking action. If *I'm confused* about the next right step, I don't have to do anything. Maybe it is appropriate to take some time for particular decisions, especially when it involves relationships. Sometimes doing nothing is the best decision and waiting to get clarity can be a brilliant idea. Perpetually staying confused about something keeps us stuck. There is more accessible information available now than ever before. We can find the answers. Clarity releases

CO-CRAZY REMINDER

Clarity gives us the freedom to take action when we see the truth. Denial is the opposite of clarity. Sometimes we resist clarity because we are afraid of the truth.

energy and promotes forward motion. Confusion is another way we allow our fears to control us.

All of these expressions are ways to not address the initial pain of setting boundaries in our lives. If we minimize our feelings and thoughts about something, we don't have to face speaking up and maybe seeing someone's disappointment. We may have different beliefs than our spouse, family, friend, or child on a particular issue. This is how the world works, but many of us don't feel the freedom to speak up for ourselves or express what we honestly think or feel. We are crippled by what others think, what others feel, people getting angry at us, being disappointed in them, making a mistake, not being perfect, and then not loving us. Working on being more okay with your truth and learning how to set boundaries is an essential skill to put into action if you want clarity, self-esteem, and peace.

Tips for Working with Fantasyland

- Begin to practice sitting with your thoughts for five to fifteen minutes. Just notice. Find some form of meditation that works for you. The idea is to start getting comfortable with your thoughts moving in and out, not reacting, or needing to act on them.

- Notice if/when you are judging or getting defensive— look at the context.

- The same goes for obsessive thinking. Notice what happened right before the obsession got activated— look at when the underlying feelings began.

• Breathe. Practice doing ten deep breaths three times a day. Five counts in, hold for five, and seven counts out. Notice what it is like to be still.

Questions to Dive Deeper

1. Look at the automatic responses you have to people. Begin to be aware of your automatic judgments and stories you make up about people you don't even know. Remember, they are just thoughts. Where do they come from?

2. What are your obsessions? If they are a way you stay distant from yourself, what are you avoiding? What underlying feelings, wounds, and beliefs are you trying to escape from?

3. What do you make up about yourself and others to stay small and stuck?

4. What is getting in the way of living a bigger, more fulfilling life?

5. Who is the judge in your head who is continually talking, assessing, and trying to feel "better than" so your true self can feel safe. Is this the real you or some voice you inherited?

RECOVERY:
Jumping Off the
Crazy Train

"We are all Warrior KQWeens: the king, the
queen, masculine/feminine, courageous,
bold, vulnerable, compassionate, dazzling,
surrendered, willing, fierce, loving, kind,
whole, blessed, expansive, beings of lights—
you've got this."

—Coming Home to Ourselves Group

16

Setting Boundaries: Time to Get Yourself Back

When we can learn to tolerate feelings while setting boundaries, it's a game changer. The fear of hurting someone we love or anyone we are connected to can cause an internal struggle that creates resistance to setting clear boundaries. We have no idea of this great cost to our well-being. Having clarity in this vital task can reduce anxiety, depression, low self-esteem, rage, and the disconnect to self and others. When we can put ourselves first with this fundamental behavior, it creates a sense of ease and wholeness in our emotional and relational worlds. Setting boundaries takes courage, self-love, trust, and the belief that your sanity and serenity are the most critical aspects of your life.

The first step in learning to set boundaries is to begin noticing where there are boundary violations in your life. We can get so familiar with people's behaviors that we don't recognize the inappropriateness until we can become aware of our feeling states. One sign that someone is crossing our boundary is when we experience anger. Anger can be a great motivator to begin to set clear boundaries. Sometimes it takes acknowledging and experiencing the anger about a situation that will lead us to take the action needed to set a boundary.

We learn how to set boundaries as we grow and develop by the example of our parents. If our parents don't have any awareness of their own boundaries, it becomes our job to decide what feels right, but we may not feel safe enough or have the inner power to speak up.

Some examples of inappropriate boundaries in my early life were:

- My father continually talked to me about his relationship with my mother.
- My father barging into my room without asking—even when I was a teen changing my clothes.
- Active addiction in the house.
- Relentless screaming and yelling.
- My parents both walking around in their underwear.

These were all boundary violations. Their problems were our problems. It isn't appropriate for a child to hear ongoing updates about their parent's relationship. Kids want to feel safe and know that their parents are doing their jobs. What often happens when parents aren't getting along is that a mother or father will inappropriately rely on a child for their emotional needs to be met. It is an enormous burden for children because kids do not want to be worrying about their parent's relationship. As parents, it is our job to find peers or professionals to resolve our issues, not to put the burden on our children.

My father and mother speaking to me endlessly about their relationship led me to feel responsible for their well-being. This was the beginning of my co-crazy. It took the focus off my own life and on to my parents' issues. The expectation that I could solve my parents' relationship problems when I was ten years old is insane for a kid to even contemplate, but sadly it became the preoccupation of my existence. The desperate goal driving me was the belief that if I could heal them, then I would feel okay.

The fact is that they were the only ones who could fix their relationship. Moreover, I continuously got more and more resentful that this was happening. My anger was unconsciously managed in multiple ways by overeating, people-pleasing, staying busy, and focusing on everyone else so I didn't have to experience my underlying feelings. I did not feel like I could speak to them about it, so a pattern of repressing my feelings began. These are some aspects of the co-crazy dynamic as a result of inappropriate boundaries: being consumed by fear and anger, avoiding feelings, and detachment from one's self. There are numerous reasons why it is challenging to speak up and set boundaries or ask for what we want or need, but it always comes back to underlying fears.

The main fears that got in my way of setting boundaries were:

- Fear that someone would get upset or angry.
- Fear that I would hurt their feelings.
- Fear of losing their love.

These fears that have already been operating since childhood lead to the hesitancy to set boundaries in adulthood. When I continuously accept behaviors that aren't acceptable and I can't speak up, it's easy to start feeling co-crazy. We struggle with wondering, *Is it me or them?* We become stuck between what we want and what someone else wants, which makes us confused to identify our own needs. Frequently, it's too scary to face our fears and set a needed boundary. We may be preoccupied with the consequences of our potential actions. We often stay blocked in silence due to projecting that the status of this relationship will shift if we express ourselves honestly.

The deadly cost of not taking this step is that we sacrifice the relationship with ourselves. When we are preoccupied with another's response to us, it makes it impossible to speak our truth. We are crippled by this unconscious fear of the ultimate imaginable consequence. Our thoughts and feelings and our real truth remain spinning in our head with no place to go. This creates unrelenting rumination and obsession. This withholding leads to internalized shame, anger, more fear, confusion, and increasingly low self-esteem. This also creates a disconnect in our relationships because we are unable to be honest with others. The cumulative tragedy becomes that our fears lead us to stay silent, which results in losing both the relationship to ourselves and the relationship to others.

Early in sobriety, an example of fear running my ability to say my truth in what seemed like a simple situation was my inability to pick out a restaurant. My date would say, "Where would you like to eat?" I would reply, "I don't care." My date was giving me the opportunity to state a preference of where I wanted to eat, but I would be terrified of his reaction to my choices, thus I dismissed my own needs. I was reacting from the past with old fears with my father, so I was fearful of upsetting my date even though he had never given me a reason to be afraid. When I needed to say something important to my father, it often took me a long time to be able to recognize what I wanted to say, let alone ask for a need to be met. I would be preoccupied with the fear of losing his love or feeling rejected or abandoned. It was not about my date.

We think being clear with our boundaries will cost us the relationship based on fears from childhood. The truth is, we can't have true connection if we are not willing to express ourselves even if someone may get upset. Setting limits gives people clarity in the relationship, whether the boundary upsets them or not. Boundaries set clear expectations within a relationship. It is the silence that leads to miscommunication. When we can take a risk to ask for our needs to be met in a relationship, we realize this is a normal part of an intimate connection. If we aren't clear with our boundaries, then we live in the delusion that if we continue to do a particular behavior rather than speak up, we can control the behavior in another.

Growing up, I had not learned that my needs were important, that what I had to say was also important, and that I had choices, including saying no. We participate in behavior to try to control someone else's feelings or ameliorate our fear. The ultimate expense of this behavior is that every time you do something that you know is not right for you, it chips away at your self-esteem and self-worth. This increases your level of fear and anger. It's an endless cycle. When you are participating in behavior out of fear, it not only doesn't work for you—resulting in resentment and dishonesty in the relationship—but it also doesn't work for the other person.

Returning to my previous example, if I say I don't care what restaurant we go to and then my boyfriend finds out I don't like Indian food but we have been going to an Indian restaurant, how would he feel? He would feel confused and find it hard to trust me. If you are in a relationship where your partner wants you to be honest but you are lying to save him from having feelings, this will result in endless conflict internally and/or externally. We are lying because we don't want to feel uncomfortable by saying our truth due to the fear that they may abandon us. It isn't about him. The lying perpetuates the disconnect in the relationship. The twisted belief is that I'm actually saving them from being upset. Another big lie. All me. Learning to set clear boundaries is about sitting with being uncomfortable for a while. There is a saying in recovery from co-crazy that when we begin to feel guilty after we set a boundary, we are on the right track. New territory.

Another example of not being able to express a boundary happens with sexual behavior. For years early in sobriety, I was afraid of saying no to sex. I would be dating someone and when they were ready to have sex the decision was made. Even if I didn't want to have sex at that moment, I was afraid to say no. It didn't even feel like an option to say no. Moreover, I felt like my sexual behavior could control how my date felt about me. I thought, *If I have sex, my date will care about me.* Lie. There may be a correlation. Sex and love *may* go together, but there is not a causation. Just because I have sex with someone, that has nothing to do with if they love me. I cannot control how they feel by my behavior, but this happens all the time with women. We think we need to sacrifice or deny an aspect of ourselves to get what we want, but the reality is that, once again, we lose ourselves and the honesty and authenticity in the relationship.

When I began setting limits with my dad or with men I was dating, it was stomach churning and skin-crawling unbearable. After setting a limit, I would feel sorry for my dad at times because I was violating the earlier unconscious agreements of the dynamic in our relationship. This is yet another reason we can continue to have no boundaries in adulthood: because we feel bad for the other person. We get hooked into believing that we are going to somehow destroy them by taking care of ourselves. We feel like we have the power to annihilate them but forget that they are responsible for their own feelings.

They are responsible for their feelings. Yes. Repeat.

At these moments, when we lie or omit the truth, we are not experiencing the present. The past is controlling us. It's a familiar dynamic with co-crazy where we are conflicted about setting boundaries because a plethora of feelings assaults us. One minute we feel angry, then we are afraid, then we feel bad for the other person, then we hate them, then we hate ourselves, then we feel resigned, and then we say, "f**k it!" and either overreact or don't do anything.

Setting a boundary pushes us up against our greatest fears and our most intense anger, making it difficult just to breathe, let alone speak. If we can acknowledge and notice all that goes on when we are faced with setting a boundary and do it anyway, we will begin to feel a sense of wholeness. We will increase our emotional well-being when we can transition out of our adaptations and protections to move toward being our authentic selves. If we can get some courage stirred up and pray for willingness, then we can do something different.

Another form of a boundary violation is making someone feel guilty for making the right choice for themselves. One time when I was in college, my dad called and asked me to have lunch. I was in the middle of writing a paper, and I told him I couldn't do it. He then said to me, "You don't love me?" One has nothing to do with the other. People who have been getting away with violating boundaries will use anything to keep the relationship operating in the same way. They don't want people to change or grow up because they may have to feel a loss. My father's message was that it was my job to take care of his loneliness. It is never a child's job to heal their parent's loneliness.

His behavior was about control and manipulation. Parents try to control their adult children by making them feel bad about living their lives. I've had many clients struggle with disappointing their parents by setting a boundary around what works for them. The parent has no issue giving their child their opinions, criticism, or trying to control their behaviors. The minute the adult child sets a limit or expresses a viewpoint that is different from their parents, it can result in conflict and strain in the relationship.

The same can be said for kids running the parent's life. When my son was young, we would often walk to a nearby park to play for a couple of hours. One day, there was a couple there with a four-year-old who wanted to play with my son. While our kids played together, I chatted with the couple for a while. After an hour or so, my son and I left and went on with our day. When we returned home later in the afternoon, my son wanted to go back to the park. We were surprised when we saw the same family. Their son was still running around the park, like a madman. I said to them, "Wow, we seem to come here at the same time." They replied, "Oh, we never left; our son didn't want to go home."

I was so shocked that a four-year-old was running these parents' lives. The child was obviously exhausted and needed a limit to be set. It is an extreme example of not being able to set a boundary because one cannot tolerate the feelings of another. A four-year-old may want a lot of things, but it is our job as parents to set boundaries so they can feel safe. These parents could not tolerate their own feeling states when they set the limit with the four-year-old having his own feelings. It will not help the parent or the child in the end. Eventually, the consequences of being responsible for other's feelings and not caring for ourselves lead to exhaustion, physical problems, depression, anxiety, anger, self-hatred, and a loss of self. Sadly, this list is endless.

A friend of mine, Jill, has a thirty-year-old daughter, Angela. Her daughter has tried a bunch of different jobs, been married and divorced, complains regularly to her mother, and always has a reason why her life isn't working out. Jill has a full-time job as an attorney, and I will often get a call from her: "Angela called me again and I had to stay on the phone for two hours! I'm at work. Should I answer my phone? What if it's an emergency?" I would say, "You can respond to a voicemail if it is a real emergency." Angela has been calling her mother for years with many "emergencies," that turn into two-hour conversations. Nothing has changed.

The important thing to see here is that the two hour conversations never helped Angela or Jill. What's happened is Angela gets to vent, but my friend ends up feeling depleted, angry, and behind at work, plus the anxiety of now feeling responsible for her daughter's problem. Angela is thirty, not thirteen. There is hard work going on here, so both people experience it like they are actively doing something about the problem. *Fantasyland.*

Angela needs to find a therapist and figure out how to move on. She loves making it everyone else's fault. This is the delusion Angela lives in so she doesn't have to take responsibility for her own life. Angela is the source of her own problems, but she wants her mom to fix them and her mom feels guilty about setting limits with her child. She is having a hard time letting her daughter figure out her own life. Jill's problems are about Jill, not about Angela's calls. Jill's problem is the inability to set boundaries and then to feel her feelings of discomfort and tension. Period. Boundaries would help both people get unstuck, change, and grow.

This relationship dynamic is beneficial to no one. It doesn't help the adult child because she won't learn how to work through her issues on her own and feel mastery through failures and successes. For Jill, she begins to obsess about what she could have done to cause her daughter to be this way. It activates her own guilt around her parenting, which leads to her need to continue the pattern of trying to solve her daughter's problems. Both people can use this dynamic to avoid what is truly going on in their own lives. This is when it's time to get honest, find some courage to set those boundaries, and let other people grow up and learn to tolerate their feelings. Give people the dignity of figuring out solutions to their own lives, especially if nothing you are doing is helping.

Growing up, my father had no awareness of boundaries. He wanted to do what he wanted without considering how other people felt—especially with women. He was extremely impulsive when it came to touching women or speaking to them. Due to his age or to his position of power, many women often just smiled when he was inappropriate. At the end of his life, when he lived in an assisted-living complex, he had no idea that it was inappropriate to continuously pat his nurse's bare leg while she was helping him.

When I was a teenager, I was heavy, and most of the weight I carried was in my hips. For some reason, my father thought it was his right to slap me in the ass or put his hand down the back of my pants every time he walked behind me. This infuriated me. For years, I ignored my feelings. I rationalized, laughed, and tried to avoid him. That changed after I had been sober for a year or two. My parents had a huge Thanksgiving dinner with all my brothers and their spouses, and I had been working in therapy on setting clear boundaries. Early in sobriety, I had already told him not to contact me for several months, until I was ready to speak to him after recognizing our dysfunctional relational dynamics. I was practicing putting myself first and not being responsible for his feelings.

During this Thanksgiving holiday, I stood up to help my mother clear the dishes. I went to clear my father's plate, and he slapped me on the ass. Suddenly, years of rage churned in my chest. I needed to stop this behavior. I could no longer drown my anger in a bottle of booze. Enraged and seething, I slowly and clearly stated, *"Do not touch me there. Never, ever, ever touch me again. Do not do that ever again and stop slapping me on the ass."*

My father looked shocked and confused. My body was vibrating with energy being released. It was anger that had been repressed and stored for years. It was no longer acceptable to be treated this way. I knew at that moment that my father would never touch me again without my consent. He literally stumbled over some words like, "Well, of course, I won't." He was oblivious to how this affected me. He had been participating in this dance with me for years. The only possibility of change occurring was if *I* spoke up. He did not see it as inappropriate. I had to own my anger. Find my voice. Get some courage. Set the boundary.

I began to realize that I had the power to decide what was acceptable and what was not. For years, I had been so focused on other people's feelings that it took me a long time to be able to set a limit. We fear hurting others, but it is more about tolerating our feelings when we set the limit. We can set boundaries in regards to our personal space, communication, physical contact, behaviors we will or won't do, and what we will or won't accept. Give it a try. You've got this.

Tips for Setting Boundaries

- When you are starting to set boundaries, practice with easier relationships.

- When someone asks you to do something, you don't have to answer right away. You can say, "Let me think about it" or "I'll get back to you."

- Don't give advice unless asked. When we see people falling apart, we want to control or fix them. What we learn over time is that most of the time, people just want to vent.

- When someone calls you with their latest emergency, breathe, remember that it is not your emergency, and say, "I'm sure you will figure this out" or "I'm sorry you are going through this. It sounds challenging." Then cry if you need to cry but don't try to fix it for them.

- We waste a lot of our time trying to "help." This is going to sound harsh but sometimes helping is hurting.

It is only done because *you* can't tolerate the underlying feelings. It's hard to sit with someone who is in pain and just encourage and listen without needing to take some kind of action.

Questions to Dive Deeper

1. What is so scary about speaking up? What is the underlying fear that gets activated? What do you think will happen?

2. What is the cost of allowing someone to violate your boundaries, whether it is by their addiction, speech, dismissiveness, or other unacceptable behaviors?

3. What are you afraid of losing by setting a boundary?

4. What is the real truth behind not setting boundaries? (Ex.: I get to be the good guy, I get to be a hero, people will love me, etc.)

5. Where do you violate other people's boundaries by trying to control them?

17

I'm a Control Freak

I'm a recovering control freak. Notice the word recovering, not recovered. The word control gets confusing because people may picture someone needing to dominate another person—maybe a scary, angry person, or a parent or a boss telling you what to do. There are numerous ways people try to control others, some of them conscious and some not. A stereotypic example of control is a husband controlling a wife or child through intimidation, but that is not the control I'm referring to.

The type of control I'm talking about is much less noticeable. Due to our fears, we are continuously trying to control the world around us. This is illustrated by our behaviors and the way we speak to others. By this definition, we may utilize numerous ways of being or ways we communicate with others to try to control outcomes. These are behaviors learned in early childhood to manage our environment in order to feel safe rather than anxious. Our underlying fears lead us to want to *feel* in control at all times even though the reality may be otherwise. These old behaviors are fighting a losing battle. They keep us living in the delusion that this way of behaving gets us what we want, but all they really do is negatively affect our relationships.

When I first got sober, I was afraid of not getting my needs met, which led me to try to control everything. I lived in a chronic state of anxiety and believed that if I wasn't in charge, the world would fall apart. I couldn't trust my environment to guarantee a feeling of safety. I couldn't trust others to meet my needs. This resulted in maladaptive controlling behaviors of micromanaging my environment. For example, I would go out to dinner with a group of six people after a meeting, and the next thing I knew, I was acting like a stage director in a play, saying "Johnny, tell us that story about . . . " or "Elizabeth, share with Dave what happened to you the other night with that guy."

It is embarrassing to admit because I was trying to just hang out with people, but this behavior was the way to ease my own anxiety. Even though I had no idea how others were feeling, I was preoccupied with them being happy or having a good time and believing that it was my job to make that happen.

Until we start to break down the fear, we don't even realize we are controlling. Usually, people around us tell us before we know it. They would say to me, "Just let her talk already." When you grow up feeling like you're on your own, you learn lots of ways to get what you want. I was a people pleaser extraordinaire and was driven by the need to have people like me so I could feel safe. I didn't realize that I was acting out earlier ways of survival, and these behaviors represented the core of how I interacted in relationships.

The people-pleasing was a controlling behavior due to the fear of just being me. I was a people pleaser because I was afraid of speaking my truth and asking for what I needed. I was really just scared to sit with my feelings and let other people be themselves. If we are stuck in people-pleasing behavior, we aren't

CO-CRAZY REMINDER

Let people have their feelings. It is not our job to manage other people's feelings. It is our job to be a witness and be present when people express how they feel—that's it.

being true to ourselves. We are attempting to influence how someone feels about us by being who they want us to be. This dismissal of our real self creates the disconnect to our true feelings, leading to our ongoing behaviors to protect ourselves. We are driven more by a need for validation and approval rather than a solid sense of self. Remember: Nobody is pleased.

People-pleasing was one of the ways I tried to control my relationships. There were also many others: lying, manipulating, avoiding topics, passive participation, aggressiveness, pretending, being seductive, acting out with anger, avoiding conflict, and more. We use these behaviors because we don't believe we will get what we need without them. The cost is we lose our relationship to ourselves. We sacrifice the connection to knowing what we think and what we feel because we believe we can't be our true selves.

One of the most extreme examples of co-crazy controlling behavior is thinking that we can get someone sober. We can only influence their decision by what boundaries we set with them, but we can't do it for them. After working with people with substance abuse problems for years, growing up with an alcoholic, and marrying two people in recovery with one of them relapsing, I have finally surrendered to the fact that I am powerless over other people and their behavior. Okay, don't freak out on me. I am only powerless over their behavior. I am not powerless over my own behavior.

There is a big difference between saying to someone, "Look, I know you're suffering, but I can't have you living in my house anymore. If you can't get sober in the next two weeks, I need you to leave" and "I can't stand your drinking anymore. When are you going to get sober, you are driving me crazy. I can't believe how much money I've given you. You need to go to an AA meeting!"

One style of communication is to let someone know what *I* am going to do. It has nothing to do with the other person. I can tell them the actions that *I* am going to take. Again, it is about being able to tolerate what happens inside of *us* when we set boundaries. Some people may not be happy with what we are saying, but we are not responsible for their response. This is a huge step toward freedom and recovery from co-crazy. Again, the mantra: I am not responsible for other people's feelings, thoughts, and behaviors. Repeat.

The alternate (co-crazy) way of communicating is focusing on the other person and what you want *them* to do. Back to that losing battle. All this does is create conflict and resentment in the relationship. Communication in the formerly mentioned way of keeping the focus on yourself is not easy, but it's more effective than living in chronic conflict. I have seen people fighting for years over what one wants the other person to do rather than expressing what *they* are going to do. This is where the addict is not the one with the problem. The one with the problem is the person trying to control the addict and their addiction. This is an excruciating relationship dynamic because underneath it all is the fear of losing a loved one.

My husband struggled with his addiction for several years. He lied, manipulated, cut back his drug use, changed jobs, took meds, and was in and out of twelve-step meetings, but he couldn't stop using. More importantly, I needed to stop my own delusion of control, which was thinking that I could control him and his substance use. Early on, I could *not* set the limit and ask him to leave. I kept wanting him to get better, so I became more and more controlling, telling my husband that he needed to go to meetings, holding on to his medications, making therapy appointments for him, and telling him to call his sponsor.

This is where we are trying to "help," but it doesn't work and just makes both people worse. He didn't want to get sober; he just wanted me to stop bugging him. *I* was the one losing my mind, not *him*. I did not become a controlling person because I was married to an addict, but it did make me much worse. The more fearful I became, the more controlling I got. The addict and the co-crazy are the same because underneath the addict's substance is the same fearful person as their partner who is trying to control them. Both are driven by fear in equal measure.

Being a parent is an excellent opportunity to practice control-freak recovery because parenting is scary. Most people don't get to practice doing it before it happens. It is a great way to practice self-awareness, especially when we are afraid and subsequently want to control our child's behavior. And we are scared a lot. The following example is a way I coped with the desire to control a situation but then realized it was about my fear.

My son wanted to have a Super Bowl party. It was going to be eight of his closest pals all hanging out in the living room, screaming, yelling, having fun. No big deal, right? For some reason, the week before this happened, I started thinking it was a bad idea. I began dropping hints about the game being on too late and the house being too small. I wanted to control an event but it was really about controlling my feelings. He didn't buy it. Before I let my distorted thinking take over and tell him he couldn't do it for some lame reason, I took a different approach.

I did an exercise around my fear and what was coming up for me, which had nothing to do with my son and his friends. It was all to do with my own past life experiences. It may sound like a small thing, but I was experiencing severe anxiety about this party, so I knew it was not about the present situation. Fear leads me to controlling behavior, which negatively affects my son. My physiological reaction of anxiety was due to past trauma that had been activated. The fear that was activated from earlier memories led me to the need to act out controlling behavior, which could have been telling my son he couldn't host the party.

I worked it out through writing and shared with Max some of my anxiety. He was able to review all the things he would be responsible for and exactly what would happen. When we looked at the facts, it reduced my anxiety. This may sound nuts, but fear is fear. This dynamic between parents and kids happens all the time. I've seen how parents' unfounded fears lead them to limit their child's life experiences. Take a look at your own scenarios like this. It is important. The party was awesome!

When we identify ways we are controlling, we can begin to change. First, we have to tolerate our own feeling states. Then we can acknowledge the underlying powerlessness and fear that was underneath the need to control. We have now begun to touch our vulnerability and humanness. We can have relationships where we don't have to live in constant fear. We can feel our power again by seeing that we have choices. We don't have to wait for someone else to change.

List of Ways We Try to Control People:

- Manipulate
- Threaten
- Yell, get angry
- Passivity
- Passive/aggressiveness
- Avoidance
- Silence/depression
- Physical problems
- Creating constant crises
- Threat of abandonment/pulling away love
- Constantly telling someone what to do, how to do it
- Chronic criticism
- Acting out/addictions
- Financial control
- Shaming others/blaming
- Sarcasm
- Nagging, bugging, pestering
- Giving unwanted advice
- Doing things for them that they should be doing
- People-pleasing

- Shutting down
- Avoiding them
- Not having sex
- Controlling with sex
- Staying in a state of denial
- Not accepting reality

Tips to Change Your Controlling Behavior

- Start to recognize where you may be using controlling behavior.

- Look at the go-to way you try to control others. (None of us wants to see that we are controlling. Remember, no self-judgment, just assessment.)

- Take a minute to honor and embrace your inner kid who decided she needed to figure this out or she wouldn't survive. Tell her she doesn't have to feel afraid anymore. She is getting herself back, and she has the freedom to choose how she will interact with people.

Questions to Dive Deeper

1. What are the underlying fears leading to the controlling behavior?

2. Where do the fears come from if they are not about the present situation? What feels familiar about this situation? Is the level of fear equal to the experience that is happening now?

3. What are some leftover strategies you used as a child that may not be working now?

4. What are some new tools you could use to cope with the fears that lead to controlling behaviors?

Leaving Crazy Town

Accept, Surrender, and Let Go

"Acceptance is the answer to all my problems today."
—Alcoholics Anonymous

These can be the hardest concepts to embrace when we have issues with control, but they can also be the most powerful. When I am struggling with resisting something or I'm in conflict with someone, the only way to find the solution is to surrender (silent scream, "What powerlessness?"). The more I try to force a solution or try to convince someone to see my perspective, I get more and more twisted up. When I decide to stop struggling there is different energy inside of me. Suddenly I have peace, calmness, willingness, and openness rather than the need to participate in an argument.

I'm not saying that we shouldn't work hard to resolve things with people. This distinction is when the struggle, angst, and internal anxiety keep getting worse no matter what we do. Then it is time to surrender, step back, and reassess. Often, when we slow down, take a break, or feel the energy of surrender, the answer comes to us. I know when I'm choosing my will over God's will by whether or not I'm in conflict. If things are going smoothly and things seem to be falling into place with little effort, I know my will is lining up with the universe. When I am trying to change someone else's mind or in a debate with my son over something ridiculous, the answer is to surrender. Continuing to battle when no good can come from it is a waste of time, but I can get attached to being right or being in control of an outcome.

This is a skill that becomes more fine-tuned over the years, so don't be hard on yourself if you forget to take these pauses at first. I eventually was able to discern when something was God's will—or felt right, however you want to say it—by my inner compass. I would feel this flow moving in my chest as if I was being pulled along to the next thing. There was no struggle or conflict; instead, there was an ease. I went through many challenges trying to figure out what was the right thing to do. Surrendering, accepting my powerlessness over others, and trusting I would be guided was a perfect place to start.

Acceptance is a powerful word. Often we get so wrapped up in the insanity, or co-crazy, that we don't even realize we lack acceptance. Sometimes we feel more in control over something if we stay in the struggle. Accepting certain things may take a long time. Acceptance doesn't even mean we have to like it or agree with it. It means we are finding peace within ourselves regardless of the outside issue. Accepting something we have done, or something someone else has done to us, or where we are at this phase of our lives—all of these things can feel like you are giving up, but it is where you will find your power.

Being self-reliant from a young age means that surrendering or admitting powerlessness were not my go-to. It was always more about trying to make or force something to happen, no matter what. "Back me up, God—I'm going in" was another mantra. My feisty determination has brought me successes. At times though, this determination can border on trying to control an outcome rather than surrendering to what is. I can do my part, but then I have to let go of the results. This is the peace that only comes with surrender.

When I can continuously surrender each morning to a power greater than myself, I can let go of the striving and effort and just do the next right thing. This is the difference between allowing the day to unfold before me and trying to force an outcome because I'm afraid. Acceptance is not about just sitting back and letting everything happen. You have to participate in your life. God can only steer a moving ship. There is a sweet spot between acceptance, powerlessness, and effort.

18

Co-Crazy Communication 101

One of my clients told me a story about how he avoided getting in trouble when he returned home after a three-day bender. He said that the minute he arrived home and his wife opened the door, he would immediately verbally attack her. He would start saying things like, "Why would I come home to a house that looked like this?" "Of course I was gone—how could I live with someone like you?" "I cannot believe you are giving me a hard time. Why would I come home when someone yells at me?" On and on it would go. What would happen? His wife would apologize. Yes. This is an extreme example of co-crazy communication and manipulation.

This sounds brutal but it happens all the time to different degrees. Tension and conflict escalate quickly, and the fight

CO-CRAZY REMINDER

When you are dealing with an addict, alcoholic, or anyone else who doesn't want to take responsibility for their lives, their best strategy is to attack and take the focus off themselves.

179

begins rather than confronting the real issues at hand. Fact: My client came home after being away for three days drinking and drugging and treated his wife horribly. When we are in the co-crazy, we have a survival reaction to fear. Both people start playing their roles to get through the most recent crisis, and then they go to their corners and hide in denial until it happens again. The trouble is that most of us don't like conflict, so we will do anything to avoid it. We continue to compromise, sacrifice ourselves, and dismiss our needs in order to keep the peace.

Nothing ever gets resolved. Nobody is listening, both parties are reacting with fear and anger, and neither person knows what their true thoughts and feelings are because they are stuck in survival mode. When treating couples over the years, I saw that problems with communication, and more specifically not learning how to listen, were the leading causes of pain and frustration. Often, by the time a couple came in to see me, they were ready for a divorce, and both people were hurt, angry, resigned, and defensive. This was a hard place to start.

I am not an expert in couple's therapy but I did see couples and families in which addiction was present. Addiction is a disease of relationships. Even though addiction is the act of one person, it affects many lives, like a tidal wave coming to shore. Part of the problem with working with addiction is we want to blame the addict, rather than seeing everyone's participation in the broken family system. It is challenging to see our part due to the consequences of accumulated deep hurt and resentment between spouses or families. But we have way more power than we think.

It's incredible to think about how none of us learn crucial communication skills. What a benefit it would be if it were taught to kids in high school—how to listen, empathize, and validate someone else's experience. We all want to feel heard, understood, and acknowledged. It seems simple, but how we communicate is so interwoven with our past wounds, beliefs, and resentments that it is often impossible to listen. Most of the time, folks just want their experiences, thoughts, and feelings validated—that's

CO-CRAZY REMINDER

Having a relationship is not about fixing someone; it's about loving them. Give them the dignity to fix themselves. Don't allow someone in their crazy to ruin your day or even ruin your life.

it, nothing more. They don't need advice, interpretation, or suggestions. They just need someone to be present while they speak their truth.

Learning how to communicate effectively is a wonderful skill to learn in and of itself. Learning how to communicate with someone in their crazy and not get entangled in the insanity is another issue altogether. Several tools work brilliantly, starting with something called "Don't take the bait," which is a common phrase in twelve-step programs. Taking the bait is getting hooked by someone who wants you to get involved in their drama. Examples are: my client coming home and his wife reacting; any substance abuser who says something to activate their loved ones; teenagers provoking their parents; spouses who externalize everything by blaming and don't take responsibility . . . the list is endless.

If you get over-involved in whatever another person is emotionally expressing, then you are taking the bait without thinking if it's reasonable, right, or accurate. A less dramatic personal example would be my college-age son coming upstairs at six p.m. from playing video games and saying, "What's for dinner?" He knows I haven't cooked anything, knows I've given him money to go to the market, and knows I've communicated clearly about when I'm cooking and when I'm not. This is his way of saying, "I'm hungry, I wish there were food, I don't want to take responsibility," so he unconsciously throws out the bait to see what will happen.

When he first came home from a semester away, I felt guilty about not cooking so I was constantly cooking and putting things in the refrigerator. I soon realized he wasn't eating any of it! He wanted his independence. He wanted to make his own decisions about food but was ambivalent about taking respon-sibility. At first when he threw the bait out, I would think, *Oh, man, he is right. I should cook more.* After realizing it was just a game, I communicated clearly with him about what I would and wouldn't do and let him have his feelings about it. This is the hardest thing for parents—letting our kids have their own experiences. So last night when he came upstairs and said, "What's for dinner?" I said, "I'm not sure, what are you planning on having?" Done.

That's a minor example of this type of communication, but it can be crazy-making and can create underlying resentments for both people. People can make us feel guilty about anything if they know us well enough. You have to admit to yourself that your spouse, children, and relatives know exactly what your but-tons are because they helped put them there. The degree to which the emotional intensity is communicated correlates with how hard it is not to take the bait. This skill will make your life much easier when you are not responsible for the behavior of the people around you.

Tips on Working to Staying Present

- Practice sitting quietly and meditating for five to fif-teen minutes. This will help you when big emotions come at you and you need to press the pause button. Practice resistance to reacting or fixing, and pause for two minutes before responding.

- Practice empathizing with someone and validating their experience, even if you don't agree with it. Just listen and notice your feelings.

- Respond to people so they know you heard what they said rather than how their story affects you. Remember what comes out of their mouths is about them, not you. Practice setting boundaries if something doesn't feel right.

Questions to Dive Deeper

1. Who in your life throws out the most bait? How do you typically respond?

2. How could you improve the way you communicate? What are some strategies to use so you don't immediately react?

3. What is painful about sitting with your feelings and *not* responding to another person's crisis? What makes it so hard just to listen?

4. What are you avoiding by keeping your life in a chronic crisis? What is *not* being said in relationships that keeps you creating drama to avoid the truth?

Leaving Crazy Town
Stop the Drama

When we grow up in this kind of craziness, we can become addicted to it. When things are calm and peaceful, somehow it doesn't feel right, so some of us need to create chaos. Drama is a way to stay distant from ourselves and does not help anyone. The only reason we need to do this is that it may be too painful not to. We may not be able to feel whatever is going on in the relationship, or we can't accept a behavior or an emotion we are feeling, and it becomes easier to distract, point the finger, blame, struggle, or blow up. It is often not even our crisis but seems to arrive on our doorstep like an unwanted present, but we still unwrap it.

CO-CRAZY REMINDER

Life is not a 911; it just may feel like it at times. Stop and think: Is this a crisis? Whose issue is it really? Mine or theirs? Is the feeling of overwhelm equal to the events that are happening? What is the reality?

When my dad moved to assisted living, I created a lot of drama. I didn't realize it at the time because I felt so co-crazy and fearful and alone. There was enough drama going on from him calling me five times a day, to his falling frequently, to his episodes of going to the hospital, to his latest argument with his best friend. It seemed endless. What I needed to take responsibility for was my participation and my contribution to the craziness.

I have four brothers. They are all different personality types and they all cared about my dad. When something would happen with Dad, I'd inevitably call one of my brothers to communicate something in a panic, and they would have an opinion. I would respond to that opinion by then calling another brother and venting to him. I would tell him what the issues were so far and ask him what he thought. I would agree with one brother, be hurt by another, and get angry at another. I would try to get people to side with me instead of focusing on a solution. I needed to ask for emotional support rather than spread my hurt and fear to everyone else.

What would happen due to spreading my insanity is that my brothers would then be mad at one another. Before long, one brother would get "activated." I would have four other people upset, including different brothers being upset with each other. Where did the whole conflict and chaos begin? Me. I was having such a hard time tolerating my fears about my dad's situation at assisted living that I needed relief. I could have called a friend. I could have gone to a twelve-step meeting. I could have talked to the nurse. Instead, I spread my problem to everyone else.

This is a typical relational dynamic when we suffer with someone else's pain or drama. It is difficult to contain our response or activation, so we end up spreading it to anyone who will listen. This is different than calling someone for support. This is calling someone and spreading your co-crazy like wildfire. Now everyone's upset. Eventually, I saw that I had to take responsibility for getting my brothers upset.

Here's another example:

Somebody calls you to talk over an issue they are having in their life. You don't know what they should do. You offer them advice, get more anxious, and feel guilty. You think, *What can I do?* What is happening here is the person has now given you their problem. This is not the same as general helpfulness and kindness. This is a *pattern* of behavior. You grab on to this issue like it is a new mission given to you by a commander.

Suddenly you have a focus and a purpose, and you start trying to figure out solutions. Meanwhile, the person who is having the issue now feels better because they know you are going to fix it. They may guilt you into it, or beg you into it, or cry their way into it. I see this frequently with parents of adult children who are struggling. Parents feel guilty about parts of their past parenting, so they now feel responsible for their child's problems. This is the toughest part of co-crazy—to let our adult children figure things out for themselves.

The most helpful thing you can do in this situation is to say, "Wow, seems like you're struggling. You have gone through things like this before. I'm sure you will figure this one out." Yup, I just said it. Not your business. First of all, it most likely isn't a crisis, but it *feels* like a crisis. With my dad, he had plenty of people around him to help. My overreaction to his feelings only served to spread my anxiety to everyone else and create an outer focus other than the real issue I needed to look at.

As we have seen, a major aspect of being co-crazy is we either overreact or underreact. These are common responses when we grow up in an environment that is unpredictable. My dad was someone who overreacted to the smallest things, but then when there was a big crisis he handled it beautifully. On the other hand, my mom dismissed everything as not a big deal. Most likely because as a mother, she had seen it all: illness, cuts, breaks, burns, and accidents. Nothing fazed her. But when we stayed home from school with a low fever, my dad would come

CO-CRAZY REMINDER

The hardest issue here is tolerating your feelings without needing to do anything.

in with magazines and candy treats as if we were on our death-beds. My mom just seemed annoyed.

As adults, we need to develop what our appropriate reaction may be to each situation that arises. The two extremes won't work. One extreme blows things way out of proportion and we get caught up in our own emotions. The other response is when we completely shut down as if it isn't happening. Denial is one way to cope—just don't feel it. It may have been the way we coped as children, so it's not pathological—it's learned and can be changed. However, this pain will be stored in our bodies and minds and will eventually surface in an unhealthy way. We may respond in all kinds of ways to our crazy upbringings or our own lives of addiction and co-crazy, but it is time to change the ones that are not working if we want serenity.

Leaving Crazy Town

Let People Experience the Consequences of Their Behaviors

Addiction and co-crazy are like living in *The Wizard of Oz*—nothing is as it seems. They both destroy relationships and create rage, mistrust, fear, grief, helplessness, relentless medi-ocrity, unspoken resentments, and unfulfilled expectations. Whether it's an addiction or a toxic relationship, recovery starts with us. If you are not the addict, and you are the co-crazy, stop participating in their addiction by not acknowledging it. Most people who are co-crazy don't see their part. They say to me, "Everything would be fine if my partner, child, parent, friend, business partner just got their shit together." Wrong. Again—the big lie.

Things will not be perfect, but if someone (you!) takes responsibility for his or her part, it may be the beginning of things getting better. Focusing on the other person and trying to change them by pleading, yelling, shutting them out, silence, over managing, giving advice, or controlling only makes things worse. This is hard to face. People are afraid. Afraid of change or fearful of their feelings, but mostly they're afraid to experience their loved one leaving or dying. It is a painful decision to save your own life first but it may end up saving theirs as well.

What I know from my personal experience, and with clients and twelve-step friends, is once the co-crazy person begins to set some limits, stops focusing on their partner (or other co-crazy connection), and starts taking care of themselves, both people have an opportunity for life. If you are in this struggle right now, speaking up and setting boundaries will be the hardest thing you'll ever do, but it may save both your lives. It is so difficult because we don't want to see our loved ones suffer, but really it's mainly because it is excruciating to feel our feelings and let them go. It feels like we are letting go of hope, but it is the opposite.

I have sat across from many, many stressed family members who are trying to save their spouse, parent, child, or friend. They are depressed; they are fearful; they have refinanced their house for another stay in a treatment facility that didn't work. The person with the addiction or other issues is typically just doing their thing, while everyone around them is getting sicker and sicker.

When the co-crazy chooses to focus on healing their own life, it creates space for the troubled person to make their own choices. This does not guarantee that the other person will choose life. This is the painful part. You can encourage them, you can be there for them, you can help them, but you cannot do it for them. "Helping" is the delusion that folks who are enabling someone live by.

A typical example may be parents who have a twenty-eight-year-old son living in their house. He has anxiety, depression, smokes pot, goes out with his friends drinking intermittently, and can't keep a job. The parents are spending a great deal of time worrying about him, of course. They fear that if they ask him to leave, something might happen to him. The problem is that they think they are helping him by giving him a place to live, but they are not. They are only delaying the inevitable task of this boy taking responsibility for his life.

The parents—who often are blaming themselves for his problems—become obsessed with the following thoughts: Wow, five years have gone by, he still isn't working. He is still smoking pot. Every time we confront him he gets really angry. He must be depressed. We must get him a therapist. Do we have enough money to help him? How is he ever going to move on with his life? It is awful for everyone involved.

It brings up so much internal conflict for the parents in this situation. My first suggestion would be for the parents to either get into therapy or start going to a twelve-step program. At this point, it is fascinating to me because I see incredible resistance from them to take any action for themselves. They believe that if their kid would just do what they tell him to do, they would be fine. Think about this. We sometimes question the alcoholic or addict when they say, "I don't need to go to a program, I can do it myself." You know that participating in some kind of program will help them. So why then is it not precisely the same for the co-crazy to get help? It's harder to face the facts of your own life than to focus on someone else.

A woman may focus on her husband's alcoholism so she doesn't have to look at her loneliness since her kids left home. A man may become obsessed with his son's issues because he doesn't want to acknowledge he hates his job or has not had sex with his wife for seven years. A sibling becomes preoccupied with her sister's depression because she doesn't want to see how unhappy she is in her marriage. If these behaviors worked and the other person got help, great. However, if it becomes an obsession or a preoccupation that is now affecting your own life and relationships, then it might be time to step back.

Leaving Crazy Town

Mind Your Own Business

"There are two kinds of business: my business and none of my business."
—Friend from twelve-step program

It may be challenging if you are someone who has thrived on other people's struggles, or if you're focused on others to give you a sense of purpose. I find folks getting defensive around this, saying things like, "Well, of course my daughter's choice of college is my business." It is only your business in how much money you have told your children you will be contributing—and you can decide where you are contributing. Beyond that, you can express concerns, brainstorm pros and cons, and help her figure out what might be the best place for her, *but it is her decision.* (I can hear some parents screaming at me right now.)

Part of the dynamic with co-crazy is that we believe everything that happens to the other people in our relationships is our business. We have a lot of advice, suggestions, concerns, feelings, and recommendations, even though most likely you haven't been asked. Most of the time, this dynamic is because for some reason we have become anxious about what others are doing or not doing.

This managing behavior is about our anxiety, not theirs. Sometimes, this is benign, like suggesting to someone they should try a particular type of tea because their stomach hurts. No problem. But if you begin calling the person to follow up, or bugging them about drinking the tea or what they are doing to help themselves, or you start losing sleep about *their* stomach problem or start dropping off books on herbs that help with the digestive system, it's gone too far. This scenario may sound outrageous, but this is the typical behavior of someone who is extremely fearful and wants to control others but sees themselves as "caring."

There is nothing wrong with helping someone, but if this becomes a pattern of behavior that either affects you or the other person in a negative way, then turn the focus on yourself. There is a difference between caring and caretaking. Some people are in necessary caretaking roles, which can be very fulfilling. Great. I'll continue with the previous example of being the contact person for my dad when he was in an assisted-living facility. The fine line comes when he is asking me to do something unreasonable, or I begin to believe that his mental and physical health is my responsibility. If I become obsessed with his happiness, peace, and loneliness, then I think it is now my job to ameliorate his feelings.

As one of my brothers used to say, "Dad's need is a bottomless empty well." No matter how much we all tried over the years to fill his well of loneliness, depression, despair, and anxiety, it could never happen. It was up to him. A psychiatrist once told me that my father was addicted to pain. I'm not sure if this was true, but what I do know is I couldn't fix him. In this situation, our job is to see the reality that he is declining and to grieve the loss of our dad and what we used to have. We cannot make him happy and we need to stop trying.

What's my business or my part of the equation is what I choose to do within this relationship that makes me feel balanced and okay. I figured out how much to visit and how many phone calls to make, and I did small things that brought Dad temporary happiness. I could not expect him to be any different than who he was or try to get any needs met by him. At times, I would slip into a delusion and expect him to be different and meet my needs. Just another unrealistic expectation to be unfulfilled. There were continuous reminders to not have an expectation of someone who is not capable of fulfilling it. However, sometimes things make sense intellectually, but our unconscious is still longing for something lost a long time ago. Acceptance and surrender. Again and again and again.

19

Depression and Its Relationship to Co-Crazy

Over the years most people who came to see me had some constellation of depressive symptoms, whether legitimately diagnosable or not. Whether they arrived seeking recovery from addiction or co-crazy, depression and all its manifestations revealed itself. There are numerous theories and hypotheses about what can cause depression and many books have been written on the topic. I've broken down into four categories what I have observed over the years have been the main contributors to depression: biological, psychological, sociological, and spiritual.

Biology

In 1997, my first real job out of graduate school was at a psychiatric hospital in Boston. I worked on the substance abuse unit where, coincidentally, I had been a patient thirteen years previously. Most of the time, the substance abuse patients had also been given another diagnosis such as depression, anxiety, or bipolar illness. The longer I worked there, it became disturbing to see how quickly patients received a psychiatric diagnosis. Someone would

191

be admitted one day, and the next morning a group of us would sit in "rounds" where the treatment team would meet the person for the first time and develop a treatment plan.

Under the influence of detox meds, the patient would sit with the five of us and attempt to piece together a narrative for the team. We got information on their family history, the pattern of substance use, their living situation, work status, relationships, and the most recent crisis that had brought them to the hospital. We also began working on a discharge plan because insurance companies lead the treatment plan by how many days they approve.

By the end of that half hour or ten minutes, I saw many people diagnosed with a severe psychiatric diagnosis based on very little information. One woman spoke of staying up late vacuuming, and the psychiatrist diagnosed her with bipolar illness. It troubled me how quickly a patient was labeled and given a medical intervention that resulted in taking serious medications. I would say to myself, *She might have been staying up all night doing lines of coke. Maybe she just needs to clear up first.*

When I was in treatment in the 1980s, one of the unspoken rules was that you let someone get sober for a year or so before deciding if they have another mental illness. Things have changed since then. The good news is that there have been developments with pharmaceuticals that were not available when I was getting sober. And the bad news is that there have been developments with pharmaceuticals that were not available when I was getting sober. There are many more medications available now than there were in the '80s, but it doesn't necessarily mean everyone needs them.

Many people are now prescribed an anti-depressant when they are discharged from treatment. Some research shows that taking meds helps people stay sober longer so they have a higher chance of successful sobriety. I'm not going to get into a big debate about pro-med or anti-med because it's not that simple. Anti-depressant medications have given some people their lives back, *and* most likely, meds are overprescribed for people with substance abuse disorders. I've seen too many people over the years try a medication that then stops working. Later they try another one, and then another. After a while, they are on four different meds and their depression remains. Once you get seduced into believing that your depression is *only* biological, you become powerless to change it.

When I have suggested to some clients that their depression may not only be biological, many of them didn't want to hear it. It is much easier to think that they can take a pill and everything will be fine. Think of taking a medication as a first step rather than the *only* step. Medication interventions can help, especially if it is a biological depression. The only way you know if it is a biological depression is if you try a medication and you then feel markedly better.

It isn't just depletions in neurotransmitters that can cause depression. There are many other things that affect our biology. Sometimes it can be a side effect of another medication. That has happened with several of my clients when they started a medication for another illness and had a depressive reaction, not realizing it is one of the side effects. I treated one woman who had a severe depression that came on suddenly and it was a mystery to both of us. We eventually realized that she had changed eye drop medication, and one of the side effects was depression. She changed her eye drops, and the depression lifted.

I've known many women in perimenopause struggling with a depression that seemed to come out of nowhere. Another client started a particular kind of pharmaceutical facial

CO-CRAZY REMINDER

Make sure you evaluate all other biological factors that can contribute to depression, such as thyroid issues, blood sugar, hormones, head injuries and substances. There are a lot of possibilities.

product and became severely depressed. She stopped using it. Her depression also lifted. So be careful what you put *in* and *on* your body.

My first week working at the hospital, I was given a case of a woman in her forties who was severely depressed. She was back in the hospital for another round of ECT (electroconvulsive shock therapy) treatments. I was told to take her down to the lower level in a wheelchair to get her treatment. She told me her story while I took her down in the elevator and we sat in the waiting room.

She had been drinking on and off for years and she was in an abusive relationship. Her husband had dominated her life for the previous decade. She was terrified of him. She also had a trauma history, was not in therapy, and drank to cope with her fear. When I spoke with her for a half an hour or so, I thought to myself, ECT isn't going to solve her abusive marriage or trauma. How is she ever going to heal from this depression if she keeps going back to this relationship? Moreover, how is rattling her brain going to give her the clarity to quit using substances and gain the strength to start thinking about what she needs? In my neophyte mind, this did not seem like the right solution to her problem. The doctors had tried many medications, and nothing had worked, so they suggested ECT. I didn't think this was going to work either. A comprehensive treatment plan was needed to address more than just her biology.

I have experienced two severe depressions in my life and medications helped tremendously. When I started taking Cymbalta for the first time, within two days I felt like a different person. I became hopeful and had more energy. My thoughts were more precise, and my feelings were less extreme. It proved to me that I had a depletion of neurotransmitters, but it didn't solve everything. I couldn't expect to sit alone in my house and stare at a wall and think that I would feel better.

The anti-depressants helped me get enough clarity and energy to give me the strength to take the actions I needed to get well. Over the years, I have treated many people with the dual diagnosis of substance abuse and depression. I do not have all the answers, but it's essential to look at these situations holistically. Medications may help, but if we don't take responsibility for the other aspects of our lives that contribute to our depression, we may not get the changes we want.

Psychological Contributors: Thinking and F***ing Feelings

If the biological is taken care of through medical intervention, then the next step is to assess what patterns of thinking or feeling may be contributing to the depression. Cognitive theorists focus on the ways we think that can contribute to how we feel. Things like catastrophizing, personalizing, all-or-nothing thinking, and mind-reading are all examples of a style of thinking that can contribute to depression. What helped me with certain kinds of thinking was to start creating a gentle relationship with my mind. *Again, thoughts aren't necessarily true, valid, interesting, or helpful. Please remember that.*

Thoughts are just thoughts. Books on spirituality, Buddhism, and mindfulness all helped me get some space around my thinking so my thoughts weren't directing my behavior. I could be with my thoughts and just notice them. Mindful awareness of our thoughts helps us avoid being run by the types of thinking that can lead to a reaction. This awareness helps to create a spacious relationship with your mind. The challenge can be that if you are experiencing depression, sometimes your thinking becomes negative or distorted. Thoughts like *I don't care if I'm on the planet anymore,* or *It isn't worth it* can be a sign of severe depression. When you start acting/thinking/feeling in ways that do not feel familiar, make sure you ask for help.

Negative thinking patterns can also be a result of fear and anxiety. If I can blame someone else for my problems, I don't need to own my choices. If I am negative and critical toward others, then I don't need to look at my underlying thoughts and feelings of inadequacy. I see depression and anxiety as these umbrella diagnoses, often being a general description masking underlying issues. For instance, a client has called to set up an appointment and they say they have depression or anxiety. That means it could be anything, and sometimes it is an underlying substance abuse disorder. If you have depression or anxiety, drugs and alcohol will not help. I'm sure you have told yourself, "Oh, I'm self-medicating, I need to solve the depression first." No. Substances always complicate getting a clear picture of what is going on. Some experts will disagree with me, but dicking around with substances while you are trying to solve an underlying mental health issue is a waste of time.

There are many possible underlying feelings that contribute to depression. One that I see frequently is anger. I had a client years ago who, at five years of sobriety, began to experience debilitating depression. She was on several medications, was participating in therapy, had a support system and a great job, but she was falling apart. Through several sessions, it was revealed that she was enraged with her husband. Not only that, but she was angry at herself for getting herself into her situation. (This is an example of lying to yourself out of fear by thinking, *This man will solve my problems.*) I give this example because it is a very common one.

This is the part of co-crazy where we see how relationships can affect us profoundly without one knowing it. Three years prior to this onset of depression, she had married for the third time. Unconsciously, she believed he would save her from her financial struggles and parenting conflicts and give her the life she had always wanted. When we don't have an awareness of our motives, we can see partners as the solution to our pain, our deprivations, or our insecurities. It is not their responsibility to resolve our issues, nor could they ever do so.

My client's main symptom was extreme fatigue. All she wanted to do was stay in bed. When she came to treatment, she appeared half asleep, but when she began to talk about her husband, suddenly she became animated. So I asked her to tell me the top five things that made her angry over the last several years and they all revolved around her relationship:

- He wasn't happy at his job and complained endlessly when he came home from work.

- He had a "collecting" issue (another word for hoarding). He loved to collect old cars and other electrical equipment that he promised to fix, repair, and sell, but this never happened.

- He didn't get along with her son, which was one of the reasons she got married—she needed help with parenting.

- He wasn't good with finances. (She was in denial about this initially because she wanted to be saved from her own financial struggle.)

- Their communication sucked. She never felt heard.

I'm not saying anger is the only thing that contributes to depression, but people can collapse into themselves when they experience overwhelming feelings of powerlessness, fear, and anger. She could not feel any hope about her situation. When we looked back over the progression of her declining mental health, we saw that she was trying to change him for the first two years of the relationship. She gave him books on communication, codependency, and relationships, but he wasn't interested in changing. He also drank but didn't think he had a problem, and she was in recovery. After she realized that none of her efforts to change him were working, she became severely depressed.

She saw that she had no way out of her situation and gave up. Feelings of helplessness can lead to depression if you don't see a way out. Through her fog of fatigue she forgot that *she* could do something. A big part of her didn't want to face the

CO-CRAZY REMINDER

Co-crazy depression comes when you realize you can't change another but you keep trying. You feel chronically helpless and powerless believing that if you just "figure it out" you can solve their problem, but it keeps failing. Brutal.

reality of a third failed marriage because it was too painful to think about getting divorced again. She gradually was able to take responsibility for her own situation, and started getting her energy back. With each step she took toward her own happiness, her energy would increase. There is power that comes from taking control of your own life and not being controlled by circumstances.

Grief is a normal part of being human, and grief can get confused with depression. If we don't process our grief, over time it can turn into depression. Grief isn't linear. It can be like a spiral where at first, we are in the very center, the bullseye of the storm. It's intense. We feel crushed, traumatized, and in shock. Then the spiral starts to circle around and we can breathe a little, but then it comes back intensely, but maybe not as intense as the beginning. The spiral keeps moving outward, giving us more time to catch our breath and settle in with this new reality as it circles further away from the original wound. Each time we circle, we come back to the grief from a different perspective and with a more spacious insight and a bit lighter.

It can come back to us years later when we are reminded of that person in some small way. Every time I see a particular type of Jeep, I think of my second husband. Now it brings a smile to my face and I think about the blessings we had. Sometimes, late at night when I roll over in bed, I can actually feel his skin up against me. It's a beautiful sensation. It's lonely at times, but this part passes.

When my second marriage ended due to my husband relapsing, I felt intense fear, shame, anger, and grief. I felt like my life was falling apart again. I was embarrassed that I couldn't stay married. I was fearful about making it on my own. I was sad for my son, I was sad for my husband, and I had to be careful to not slip into depression. I was also grieving. I tried to identify how I was feeling, write about it, talk about it, and reach out to people. What I felt like doing was lying around and watching movies, not talking to people, isolating, and eating Almond Joy ice cream. Temporary fixes don't work in the long run. Crap.

Social Factors

One of the most common behaviors of people who are depressed is isolation. It is often hard to know what came first—the depression or the isolation. Are people depressed because they are isolated or isolated because they are depressed? Isolation is common even with my clients who aren't depressed and it is something that, when addressed, can change someone's entire way of being. It is incredible how many wonderful people are out in the world with such little human contact. It always surprised me when I began with a new client who I thought was this wonderful human being, and then realized they had no friends. It may have been due to raising kids or being in a certain position at work or getting too comfortable staying inside—many people are not just isolated, but lonely.

Isolation can be a common result by the time someone comes to my office to address a substance abuse disorder, but the addicts in recovery aren't the only ones needing connection. We all do. It can be challenging to connect when we don't feel good. The last thing we want to do is socialize or reach out to someone when we feel down. It isn't just about connecting on a surface level. It is about somebody seeing you in a deep, profound, and authentic way. I myself have to be willing to be vulnerable, be open, and tell the truth about what is going on with me. When I'm feeling good, it is easy for me to make plans with people because I am "up" or "on." What is more challenging for me is to get together with someone when I'm not feeling great.

It isn't just about opening up when you aren't on top of your game, but it is also keeping your voice when it may be difficult to speak up. Finding your voice is critical to moving through a depressed state, even when it is challenging. This is such a common struggle for folks who avoid conflict. They don't speak up about what is important to them. Unfortunately, if you do this often enough and long enough, you will end up resentful, cynical, blaming, angry, depressed, alone, or in co-crazy relationships.

The underlying fear keeps us from being our true selves and being fully self-expressed, which leads to accepting the unacceptable in relationships. The cycle begins with the fear of speaking up, to internalizing fear and anger, to tolerating and accepting co-crazy behaviors in relationships, to again the fear of speaking up, then goes to internalizing . . . the cycle goes round and round and round, resulting in ongoing depression.

Other social contributors to a depression can be that your marriage is in conflict, you feel bad about your parenting abilities, you don't see your family, you don't have an intimate partner, you don't feel a sense of community, you don't have friendships, or you just don't feel connected to the human race. If someone comes into a therapist's office and says they are depressed and they have been in an unhappy marriage for twenty years, we may need to look at the marriage.

Part of the reason for our isolation is that we become embarrassed or ashamed if we feel lonely even though it is a feeling everyone experiences at one time or another. Many people will do anything not to be alone or feel alone because it brings up deeper feelings, memories, or earlier trauma. Sometimes when we stop, pause, take a breath, and have some alone time, we may experience some unexpected *percolations*. Being alone can activate old feelings that have long been repressed, and we need support to work through them.

If we continue to avoid these feelings by acting out in some way—rage, eating, drinking, sex, or staying permanently busy—we will remain on the relentless path of unresolved depression. Sometimes it helps just to share thoughts and feelings with another human being and get a reality check. When we are depressed, we often see the world from this small perception of reality. We forget that it is just one perception. When we can get out of ourselves enough to connect, it helps us to see others, ourselves, and the world with a greater perspective.

Spiritual Factors

Oftentimes when there are big changes in someone's life like retiring, kids leaving home, change of job, moving, or change of a relationship, we can be vulnerable to a depression. We all have to create meaning out of our lives and have a greater purpose so we have a reason to get up in the morning. If every day feels like Groundhog Day, life can get pretty depressing. Having a spiritual life can help you feel connected to others living with us on the planet and can broaden our view to seeing the world from a greater perspective.

If you aren't comfortable with the word God, you can use any word you want that feels right to you—spirit, nature, love, consciousness, beauty or The Dude as the author Pam Grout says. You can think of something you really care about, something you would put before yourself. Sometimes we get so stuck in the smallness of our little lives we forget lots of stuff really doesn't matter. We get way too upset about the day-to-day frustrations and struggles. In twelve-step programs, we use the tool of asking ourselves, "How important is it?" Very often, it just isn't.

If I can be a loving presence wherever I go, my life runs smoothly. This doesn't mean I'm a doormat. I'm kind and loving, and I set boundaries when necessary. I also need to listen to guidance wherever I find it, whether it comes through someone making a suggestion to me or a coincidental meeting with an old friend. I need to notice what is happening around me and be connected, present, and aware, not lost in my head. I met a woman once who said she had just returned from Paris. She was frustrated and depressed because during the entire trip she was pre-occupied and resentful with her brother. She was so obsessed with trying to control the outcomes of other people's behaviors that she hardly remembered the trip. Don't miss Paris.

Several years ago, I was re-evaluating my career, and some colleagues and I were debating whether to buy a counseling center. The two psychiatrists who had run it for a long time were looking at retirement. As we came closer to making a decision, I had to acknowledge what was happening around me. It was like the universe was telling me it was not a good idea. Meeting times kept changing, the lawyer who was supposed to be working for us couldn't make numerous appointments, and other people involved were changing their minds.

This opportunity that was supposed to be such a great idea and would give me new purpose was becoming a nightmare. I knew I needed to let it go, but my ego wanted it. The universe was warning me that maybe this wasn't the best idea and to take more time to assess other possibilities. Conclusion: Don't do it. When it is God's will, there is no urgency, just an unfolding. Listen to that quiet voice inside when it's telling you something. Don't dismiss yourself or your connection to a higher power. When we are in co-crazy, it is hard to sit in stillness and listen, but the answers are there. Try to begin to trust anything that brings you more peace, serenity, happiness, creativity, authenticity, vulnerability, acceptance, and surrender.

Tips for Working Through Depression

- Create a chart for yourself to assess what parts of your depression come from biological, psychological, social, or spiritual factors. Give percentages for each. If you put 100 percent biological, think again, especially if you are on an anti-depressant and still depressed.

- What are other things—substances, food, drink, hormone creams, medications, news, negative talk, jobs that drain you, *anything*—that you think may be contributing to how you feel on a daily basis? *Make a list!*

- List five things right now that are driving you crazy or make you angry. Circle two of them that you can take an action step on right now—yes, right now (and not something that someone else is going to do—what *you* are going to do). Action helps move the energy of depression. Trust me on this one.

Questions to Dive Deeper

1. What feelings do you struggle with experiencing? Grief, anger, shame? Do you feel numb, shut down,

detached, or super busy, overcommitted, and over-burdened? These extremes may mean you are not in touch with processing your day-to-day feelings. Think of ways to stop, even for ten minutes during your day.

2. Write about what you feel—no right or wrong answers here. What makes you unhappy, what is this depression truly saying to you? Are you really angry, fearful or sad underneath the depression?

3. Are you isolated? Do you have connections? How is your co-crazy relationship contributing to your depression? Is there an action you can take right now to move you out of this dynamic? What relationships in your life support and empower you? What relationships are a burden and drain you?

4. Are you resisting shifting certain relationships due to co-crazy fears about what will happen to the other person, rather than putting your sanity, truth and life as the priority?

5. Do you have a spiritual life? What do you care about? Where do you find beauty? Peace? Where do you experience perfect harmony? Are you able to be still and quiet? Is there a disconnect between how you are living and what that little voice inside you is saying?

6. Do you have a meditation practice, a prayer practice, or have you been inspired by any spiritual books? Find some readings that uplift you and read them daily.

7. Can you do one small thing today to express who you really are? What do you want to really say and how do you really want to be? One thing. Do it and see how the energy shifts.

If you don't have energy to do anything at all, then please see a professional and get assessed.

CO-CRAZY REMINDER

The bigger the disconnect between how we are presenting to the outside world and how we truly feel inside, the greater the depression. Do you. Be true to yourself.

Leaving Crazy Town
How What You Consume Impacts Your Mood

I had a client who presented with a severe anxiety disorder. He had been sober for a couple of years but was still struggling and felt like he needed to be medicated for his anxiety. We reviewed his past history and assessed his recovery program, but we didn't find any significant trauma or clear clues to the source of his anxiety. It is normal to experience some level of anxiety and fear if you are a human being on the planet, but this was crippling to him.

Then I asked him about his diet. It turned out that he drank two pots of coffee before noon. He had a major caffeine addiction but did not connect this to the fact that by two o'clock, he felt like he was coming out of his skin!

There was also a woman who consumed two six-packs of Diet Coke a day and wondered why she chronically felt like a racehorse ready for the gates to be opened. It seems obvious, but it is not because we all want the special treats that we become attached to, whether it is coffee, Diet Coke, or a particular sweet. When it is something we get pleasure from that we may need to give up or replace, we can become like bratty children. "What do you mean, I can't drink Diet Coke?" Well, I won't tell you not to drink it, but it may be contributing to the amount of anxiety you are experiencing.

I admit that I am not perfect in this area. I still have plenty of treats I use at times to manage feelings. Let's not kid ourselves. Some things may be easier to see than others.

Again, what you take in can have a big effect on how you feel. This is what I know: I once ate an entire bag (the big one!) of peanut M&M's at the movies and the next morning, I was thinking of not being on the planet. I'm not kidding, right there when I woke up, depression. Out of the blue. My body does not respond well to large doses of sugar. I can have serious blood sugar swings after downing a frozen drink from a coffee shop that can make me physically sick, so I need to be careful.

I also had breast cancer last year, so I have been working on cleaning up my diet. I have gone up and down with food and diet for years and every year it gets better. All I know is that as someone in recovery, I want to feel good. Eating healthy foods makes me feel better. I consume less meat, less sugar and caffeine, and have increased water, vegetables, and fruits. It is not rocket science and it doesn't have to be all or nothing unless you have a sugar or food addiction or a chronic condition like diabetes. You will have to decide if you're someone who can have a little or someone who needs to abstain. Trial and error and awareness will help you see that eating poorly may be contributing to any depression you may have.

Try to figure out what makes you feel better or worse over time. It is up to you. But it can be vital if your mood is affected by certain foods. To illustrate the need for a balanced approach, when I was married to Shane, he was a strict vegetarian and ate clean—no sugar or flour. I was not. I wanted to eat as healthily as possible, but I wasn't always as motivated as Shane. This eventually became a source of shame in my relationship. I ended up feeling bad about something I wasn't committed to because of someone else. I didn't know myself enough or like myself enough to make choices that were right for me. Don't make co-crazy choices just to keep the peace in a relationship. Do what is right for you.

Get support. Every time I have tried to change an eating habit, I enlist support. I will tell myself I can do it alone but then realize after months of struggling, *Gee, I may need some help.* No shame. No drama. No making up that I should be able to figure it out. There are many great apps, programs, and support tools out there that have helped me. You don't have to do it alone. Shocking.

The coronavirus is going on right now as I write this book. After the first week, I stopped watching the news because I knew it wasn't helpful and would make me anxious. I was able to get informed each morning on my state's website. I consumed the facts, not other people's fears. This is critical to sanity. We can start to feel crazy when we have an overwhelming amount of feelings and they may not even be ours! That is why the healing from co-crazy is about keeping the focus on ourselves. We can be so affected by people around us by taking in their anxiety/fear/depression and not even be in touch with what *we* are feeling.

What's most important are my mental and physical health, and making decisions that perpetuate my feelings of harmony, love, acceptance, tolerance, and compassion rather than those that increase my feelings of agitation, frustration, intolerance, and negativity. Try to be careful about what you take in and not just food and drink, but anything. If we choose to be around negative, angry people, or read or watch constant dysfunction and violence, or read and watch the insanity of the news 24/7, this will affect our mental health. It can be an overload of negative intake and it does affect how we feel daily. It decreases the bandwidth of our resources that keep us from reacting.

Begin to notice how certain information, events, people, or places affect you physically or emotionally. When you are under stress or someone upsets you, watch how you react inside and out. I love action films. I love detective novels. Is it possible that because I listen to a lot of pain and trauma with work that I like to escape to a completely different space? Perhaps. Finding balance with all we process from our outside world is quintessential to being in a calm state.

First thing in the morning, I do my daily readings, say some prayers, and take quiet time to meditate. This comforts me. I switch out authors every couple of months, but I've read some books over and over for years. I often start my day off with laughter by looking up videos of certain comedians on my computer and I watch them for ten minutes or so. There is so much going on in the world or in our lives that we can lose perspective of the bigger picture and get bogged down by the tragedies and the chaos and suffering in the world.

It is crucial to take in the joys, the miracles, and hopeful, positive information to keep ourselves from living in the space of being overwhelmed and despairing. It requires action on our part. A friend of mine used to say, "What you put in comes out when you're squeezed." So when you are depressed or struggling with fear and anxiety, be careful of all you take in. Start taking small steps toward sanity.

Leaving Crazy Town

Connect, Connect, Connect

Due to feelings of shame about our past or present situation or behaviors, we can isolate and try to fix our lives by ourselves. We tell ourselves the lies that people don't want to be bothered or we're a burden or I should be able to handle this. Isolation can contribute to feelings of depression, anxiety, or participating/relapsing with an addiction. Possibly you have lost relationships due to behaviors, chronic complaints, or attempts at control, or it may just feel safer to be alone and too risky to be with people. Perhaps you may not want to be vulnerable or let people see the real you. It's a tough and lonely place to be. You could be experiencing one of the most challenging times in your life but you feel isolated and alone.

When I was hitting my second co-crazy bottom after my husband Rob's relapse, I hadn't realized how isolated I had become. When I met Rob, I was actively participating in programs, exercising, and raising my son. I had friends and work colleagues, and I connected with family regularly. Five years later, I was sporadically attending my support groups, had lost contact with most friends, rushed home from work to hyper-manage my life, worried chronically, obsessed about Rob's drug use, neglected my needs, and ate over my feelings. Not a happy place to be. I felt like I was in hyper-drive at all times, and I was exhausted. More importantly, I was externally focused on how to support Max, manage my psychology practice, and figure out a way to get Rob help. All of my energy was going out but nothing was coming in. I was beginning to fall apart.

As I slowly came out of the despair and fog of the co-crazy bottom, I knew I needed to take action. I started setting limits with Rob by giving him some ultimatums, but I needed to save my own life. I had suddenly ended up living in this isolated, dark cave of addiction and insanity. The first step was getting a meeting list book, and I found an AA meeting five minutes from my house. I had moved to another town when Max turned five but I didn't know anyone yet. I had been so self-absorbed with my own drama that I hadn't attended many local meetings.

When I walked through the door of this small Saturday morning meeting, there were six men and one woman. This meeting was the beginning of getting my life back. I felt uncomfortable at first due to the disconnection that had happened gradually while I was trying to manage an unmanageable life. I had been sober for a long time but the co-crazy was killing me. I needed to be with my tribe, people who were on the path to healing. These folks were so gentle and kind and supportive. After I had been attending this meeting for a while, I branched out to other support groups. I began to have girlfriends again. I began to feel a part of something again. I felt hope that my life could get better, regardless of what was going on with Rob. I began to create my own life. This happened through connection.

Leaving Crazy Town

Develop a Spiritual Practice

Over the last thirty years, I have been on many paths to get to know myself and to try to live right. I have a relationship with a God/higher power that I cherish. I know there is an energy, a love, a connection that is greater than all of us. At times, I have felt so dark and in despair that it has felt like God isn't there. Sometimes I cry along with the universe when a tragedy happens that none of us can make sense of. Sometimes I'm so pissed off at God for not getting my way that I tell him/her how angry I am. At other times, I feel such peace and bliss no matter what is going on that my entire body is filled with happiness and gratitude for experiencing this gift of life.

When I started on this path of recovery, I believed in a spiritual energy but I didn't necessarily utilize it. I have gradually become more comfortable with trusting and relying on this profound relationship for guidance and love. As the journey has continued, I've read books on Buddhism, mindfulness, spirituality, Christianity, and meditation. Rob, my second husband, was a born-again Christian. This was interesting because I had previously held beliefs about this label, but he was a beautiful soul, and knowing him opened up my belief system about religious people. He bought me a Bible. We tried different churches and read different preacher's writings. It has all helped me to be who I am today.

Find a spiritual life that values all human beings. Find a spiritual program where it is about kindness, generosity, truthfulness, gratitude, love, growth, acceptance, humility, patience, and peace. Whatever it is that brings you more understanding of yourself as a human being and of others on the planet will help create serenity. Create a daily practice. There are many beautiful books about mindfulness, meditation, and prayer, so take some time to discover what resonates with you. This is about finding your own path, creating a connection to the world, being more at ease within yourself and developing a deeper meaning for your life. Practicing mindfulness and presence is a way to experience life with more awareness. I try to be more awake and aware of what goes on around me because I can easily miss life by being in my head.

Creating a loving relationship with your mind, having compassion for yourself and others, and practicing presence in your daily life brings more contentment and peace. It also helps build some resources for when the shit hits the fan. You can experience not reacting just this one time and feel the freedom and peace it brings. And the shit will hit the fan.

20

Grief

Grief can suck. It can also be a time of reflection and deep internal discovery that we rarely get. Grief is personal. It may not have stages or a linear timeline, but we all experience it at some time in our lives, and we all do it differently.

My son just went to college. On one hand, this is so wonderful that I almost can't contain the giddiness. I can put years of worrying about his future at bay, even just for a moment, while he explores a bigger world and I can begin to inhabit my own again. On the other hand, when I wake up in the morning, I'm chronically on the edge of tears, my stomach is all twisted up, and I sometimes wander around the house aimlessly. A friend of mine dropped her son at college, went home, got one of his shirts out of the closet, put it on, got in his bed, and stayed there all day. We all do what we need to do. A few days ago, I went into my son's room and looked at his old fleece blankie peeking out from underneath a pillow. The next thing I know I'm pulling it out slowly and pressing my face into the soft material with colored stars while inhaling deeply. I sat on his bed for a minute, holding that small tattered cloth against me, trying to keep still something that had long been gone.

Pictures of that little boy with the crewcut blew through my heart and mind. A movie began to run through my head, suddenly seeing him crying when I would say no, wrestling with his buddies out in the backyard, and the precious memories of cuddling on the couch watching a movie before he got too big for that. He has been the one person in my life I've been committed to. He gave me a reason to get up in the morning, a reason to be open, a reason to remember it isn't all about me, a reason to laugh hysterically when he would go on one of his hilarious comic rants, a reason to be present when someone is telling you something where you really need to listen, and a reason to have my heart broken again and again and again.

My first intense grief response was when my mom died. I was now a woman on the planet without a mother, an ontological shift. I felt different in my bones. I didn't want to be around people, I felt separate from everyone, I wanted to go inside myself and be still and stay there. This was my experience. Some people get distracted for months, some people only begin to experience their grief a year later, some people have a hard time functioning and are curled up on their couch week after week. Others go on with their lives, finding a new purpose.

I lost a mother whom I didn't have a real connection to, and I grieved what we would never have the chance to create. Some people lose partners of a lifetime. I cannot compare my grief to another's experience. It's our process, our way of coping and our pain. Our systems need to work through it with whatever skills we have. Some people are changed forever, some aren't changed at all. The miracle is that this deep pain does transform us somehow. I am a different person after every loss. I feel more rooted, more connected to the world and others in an odd way, more understanding, more vulnerable, and more compassionate. Every human being experiences loss. What matters to me is how I can process that loss and not make it about everyone else. Staying angry or sad forever will not help me. Staying in pain forever would lead to collapsing into myself and saying, "F**k it." I've had to go through the process over and over and eventually find meaning.

When Shane and I got divorced, I seemed permanently pissed off. I remember going to an AA meeting and ranting and raving about his behavior and "I cannot believe he did that" blah blah blah. A woman came up to me afterward and said, "Have you ever thought of doing the steps?" God bless her. I had just completed another fourth step inventory, so why was I still angry? I was mad because I was getting divorced, I was angry because the vision of the happy family was blown apart, I was frustrated because I wished it were different, and I was sad because of the devastation of a dream.

I realized that no matter how much work we do on ourselves, sometimes we just need to accept where we are with our grief and hopefully not hurt ourselves or others in the meantime. The anger about my divorce was part of my grieving process, and underneath it was fear and sadness. Shane has been my biggest learning tool in sobriety. I didn't want to stay angry, but I *did* need to feel it for a while. Eventually, as I kept owning and processing it, I was able to get to a different place.

Sometimes when we have a loss, it is like a game of dominos—when one gets touched, they all start to fall down. Often, when a relationship ends, I begin to remember all the other endings. My body feels a certain familiar way, and suddenly every friend who has died, a client I've lost, a parent I miss, the partner who's gone, is running through my mind like I'm suddenly on the old show *This Is Your Life*, but it's all about the losses. At other times I will have an intense grief response to something small because it is *really* about something earlier that may not have been felt.

After I asked Rob to leave, I felt like the walking dead. I had already grieved for a period before I finally asked him to leave, but months later I still felt wrecked. I attempted to keep things moving and consistent: I kept seeing patients, I focused on Max, and we adopted a couple of kittens to bring some new energy into our lives. We loved these cats and within a couple of months, one disappeared. I was devastated. I began to obsess about what happened to the cat. I wandered through the woods for hours, day after day searching for her. I cried for weeks and missed the way she would lay completely on her back with her arms and legs in the air.

I'm sure I *did* miss the cat, but the reaction seemed extreme. I had asked Rob to leave a month or two before we got the cats.

214 Sarah Michaud, PsyD

I was in survival mode. I was numb and trying to function, but losing that cat activated all the feelings I couldn't access at the time Rob left. All I know is when the tears came, I just let them. Who cares? What I know for myself is that if I just let the storm come and pass through, I feel better, I feel lighter. It may not solve everything, but I can go on with my day without that detached feeling. Allow for feelings to come when they happen. Like I said before, it is the resistance to the feelings that gets us in trouble.

Give yourself lots of space with grief—it's a unique experience based on our personal history with all our losses. Give it room and try to be aware of what's happening so you don't have to make up some lie or story about why you might be feeling a particular way. No judgments, but it is essential to get the energy moving eventually.

I've listened to countless people over the years who struggle with loss. Of course, if we are drinking and drugging, we may not feel grief until we get sober. I've listened to people who cry week after week over small things and big things—it doesn't matter. Sometimes we just need the release or feel the relief of letting our bodies and hearts let it all go. We do this more easily when there is a safe space for us to do so. Sometimes when people get sober, all the grief is just sitting there waiting.

Sometimes both the crazy and co-crazy grieve over lost time. Having intense feelings about days, weeks, or years spent participating in active addiction, or being preoccupied with someone with active addiction, can feel gut-wrenching. There can be many repressed tears over lost dreams of careers, families, relationships, or possibilities that once were tangible but are now in the past. Losses of a self you once knew but no longer recognize, losses of chances you didn't take, losses of adventures you were too afraid to risk, all add up to grief unexpressed.

There is an energy with grief. A heartbreak. A woundedness that we can either put salve on by taking care of ourselves—being gentle and honoring what we are going through—or we can go into not feeling, over-functioning, staying busy, "I don't have time for this," distraction, or whatever skills have worked in the past. This may work for a while, but if the underlying feeling isn't addressed, it gets stuck and will come out somewhere else.

There are smaller losses people experience but they can still have an impact. Like losing my guinea pig at seven years old while slowly walking to my best friend's house holding a shoebox carefully in my hands. Forgetting that if he peed, the box would get wet and the bottom would fall out and he would run into the woods to his freedom while I stood there in the shock and disappointment of a child.

All the way to the other extreme of the devastation of losing a child. Some losses we get over quickly and some we cannot ever imagine people surviving, and we will never know how they feel. That's grief.

Leaving Crazy Town

Working Through Grief

When we are in co-crazy relationships, we stay as far away from grief as possible. The ultimate fear in a co-crazy dynamic is always that we don't want to feel the grief of losing the relationship; it feels like it will kill them or us. Just stay in the moment and begin to focus on yourself—don't worry about the future right now. Remember that the more we focus on ourselves, the more the possibility of a relationship healing can occur. We fear a loss, but the damage has already happened. We lose ourselves while denying that we have already lost them. Giving ourselves space and time to cope with whatever the loss feels like without judgment is critical. We don't need harsh voices in our heads on top of the loss.

So many times in my work with clients, people become terrified of the *what if.* Yes, it is scary to think your loved one can overdose or leave or continue to participate in a behavior that is unacceptable, but that is out of your control.

Yes, it is.

Watch for these examples of co-crazy thoughts, feelings, and behaviors resurfacing during periods of grief:

Co-Crazy Thoughts:

- I shouldn't feel this way.
- Other people suffer more significant losses than mine.
- I should be able to function and take care of my family—what is wrong with me?
- Why don't I feel better already (after two weeks)?
- I'm full of self-pity. I'm being selfish and self-indulgent. Snap out of it!
- I know I can fix this.
- I must be crazy.
- What's wrong with me?

Co-Crazy Feelings:

- Guilty that you're not able to do for others like you used to.
- Depressed that you aren't able to keep over-functioning, feeling a loss of identity.
- Feeling completely uncomfortable because you are the one who needs help.
- Trying to resist and ignore that you now have needs.
- Uncomfortable that people want to help, and telling everyone you're fine.
- Not allowing people to help because you will feel like you owe them.
- Anger at everything. Overreactions to small things.
- Distracting yourself when tears come instead of letting them flow.
- Feeling crazy.
- Feeling guilty when you start to feel better, like there is a particular way this is all supposed to be happening.

- Moments of overwhelming sadness.
- Increased anxiety.

Co-Crazy Behaviors:

- Acting out in some way, like picking up a drink or a drug, or suddenly being attracted to a guy at your mother's funeral whom you knew in high school and sleeping with him. (Check!)
- Starting to push everyone away and isolate (you may need some alone time, but isolation is different).
- Making big, sudden changes like moving to Hawaii (not that anything is wrong with this), but we believe we won't feel the same way if we are somewhere else.
- Becoming obsessed about something or someone, not realizing we are just avoiding grief.

The possibilities are endless. Some behaviors are obviously helpful to process your grief. We can't just sit in it endlessly and feel. The maladaptive thoughts, feelings, and actions aren't going to help us—they keep us in fantasyland.

Tips for Working with Grief

- Whatever you feel and however you feel it and for however long you feel it is your business. Now, if it's ten years after you lose your goldfish and you are still mourning, we need to address it.
- Give yourself time. Time to feel or not, time to assimilate to a new way of being—it takes what it takes.
- Remember the spiral: at first, it's an intense wound in the middle—pain, detachment, rage, disassociation, exhaustion—however the initial impact lands. Then the spiral starts to move outward a little, but it's still

218 Sarah Michaud, PsyD

close to the center, and the pain doesn't lighten much at all. Eventually, over time, we may not feel it for a minute, or an hour, or even a day. The spiral keeps moving outward, away from the original wound, and we begin to get some space and time between intense feelings of grief.

- Get rid of anything that is not critical in your life. Get rid of anything that is draining your energy. You don't have time or the bandwidth for bullshit. Time to make a shift. Sometimes it takes something big like a loss to make some changes.

- Keep these words close to your heart: surrender, powerlessness, acceptance, gentleness, allowing, grace, gratitude, beauty, and remembering the goodness of beings.

- You can do this no matter what.

- Pray as often as needed.

Questions to Dive Deeper

1. Do you feel like you have given yourself the space and time to process your losses, or do you feel like you get busy and have denied the impact of them?

2. Do you still feel stuck in grief from a loss that happened a long time ago, but you have never accepted it or assimilated this experience?

3. Are you holding on to blame or shame or guilt around the loss? Do you need to forgive yourself or anyone else for anything?

4. What would it take to allow yourself to release the pain, hurt and holding on to the past? What gets in the way of your freedom? Are there some underlying resentments getting in the way of grieving?

21

Shame

When my son turned a particular age, I would re-experience my unresolved trauma from my own life at that age. This phenomenon happened to me frequently over my years of parenting, always leading to facing more growth opportunities. Going through junior high with him was a nightmare—for both of us. He is at college now, and it is the fall of his eighteenth year. Sometimes I feel like I'm still recovering from the fall of my eighteenth year.

In November of 1977, I moved to Miami with a friend to find a job as a waitress during the busy season. It was my gap year before I went to college, and as my dad famously said, "Go sow your wild oats." Unfortunately, my interpretation was to sleep with lots of men and snort tons of cocaine. I'm not sure this is what he had in mind. When certain events come to mind, I want to vomit. It's an automatic bodily response. Shame: that feeling of disgust with myself, the sense of wanting to be invisible or the feeling of wishing "it" never happened. The overwhelming feeling like something must be wrong with me, or never wanting to "look there" or "feel that." Forty years later, I can still remember that time and feel it deep in my bones. That shiver goes up my spine, and a voice inside my head says, "Seriously?"

There is nothing like the joys of shame. In trying to bring lightness to the dark, we often refer to it in a comical way like

219

"the spiral of shame" or "the shame train." It feels like darkness, secrets we can never, ever, ever tell anyone. I've pretty much heard everything over the years. People sharing secrets that have brought them a lifetime of shame, to finally letting go and realizing they're not alone. Especially if you're an addict, the shame leads to more addiction, which then causes shame, then addiction, and the cycle continues. Shame is also part of being human. (Here we go with the feelings again.) Nobody is perfect and we all do shit we regret. Even co-crazies.

For many people, it revolves around sex. Maybe because of all the guilt that is put on people by religion or parents or cultures. I've often read that the difference between guilt and shame is that guilt is a feeling we get when we feel bad about something we have done, and shame is feeling like *We are bad*.

It is crazy when you think of it because most people participate in sex, so why the shame? We all have a belief system around what is "good" or "appropriate," or what we are willing to do or not do. It is different for everyone. I've heard people talk about experiencing shame from not having enough sex, to having too much sex. Others talk about how far down they have gone with addiction/co-crazy that has led them to have sex when they didn't want to, or shutting a partner out for years. Both groups of people experience shame.

For women, it is often around abuse or rape, or saying yes when we wanted to say no, or sleeping with people out of a longing to be loved or wanted. Tragically, the satisfaction of that longing gets linked with our sexual behavior, or what we think is going to keep someone from abandoning us. Some women have shame that they even *experience* sexual feelings or want to try something that feels shameful. They may have shame around their bodies and that their bodies aren't enough in some sexual way. Some women have never had an orgasm and are ashamed to admit it. Some women feel like they can't have the *right* orgasm.

For men, shame can be linked to sex but also linked to violence. I have known men over the years who, when they were teens, had a mutual masturbation fest with their pals and then worried for years that they were gay. Other men ended up with their best friend or sexually confused because of a drunken night out. I've listened to men cry over heinous acts they have done to people for drugs, money, or status. Some men have shame about what they have done to others in the name of "being a man." Others have shame about their need to be controlling around sex because of a deep fear of abandonment.

For an addict, we have years of participating in behaviors that we may not have done if we were clean and sober. Once we have a few drinks or a few lines or a few pills, our decision-making process vanishes. Someone we may not have been interested in five drinks ago suddenly seems totally appropriate. The shame of that next morning when you open your eyes and wonder where you are and don't recognize the person next to you can bury us. I have had clients who had total blackouts of months of a relationship. They meet the person years later and don't remember their time together. Alcohol and drugs just increase the odds of doing something that you will end up feeling shame about.

For the co-crazy person, we may feel shame about different behaviors than the addict/other. When we participate in sexual behaviors out of fear of losing someone or getting angry, we are not in touch with what we need or desire. This leads to shame, anger, fear, and a complete disconnect with self. Once we can focus on ourselves, we may begin to feel underlying feelings of shame that have been masked for years. When we are obsessed with another person changing, it is hard to tap in to any feelings, let alone shame. We may have done things to keep a relationship, like lying or manipulating or projecting guilt onto another person so they won't leave. I've heard women crippled by guilt because of getting pregnant to keep a relationship due to a deep shame of feeling like they are "not enough" or feeling like they will be abandoned. I've listened to men confess their shame because they felt conflicted and enraged since the day this happened.

Often we have felt afraid to have needs in a relationship. Thus we want people to read our minds and get angry when they can't. We may feel shame just having needs at all. Being intimate with someone can be a beautiful, tender, loving, wild, exciting experience. It can also contribute to deep feelings of shame and regret. When I first got sober, I remember my friends and I joked that it was easier to have sex with someone than to have coffee with him. With coffee, you had to talk. Sex meant so little to me and intimacy was so scary to me that having a coffee with someone was way more terrifying. For years, sex was something I automatically did because I never thought twice about whether I wanted it or not. It was a way I could feel wanted, which of course never worked.

I love Charlotte Kasl's quote from her book *Women, Sex, and Addiction:*

> "We forget that sex is sex. And that
> sex is not proof of being loved;
> sex is not proof of loving someone;
> sex is not proof of being attractive;
> sex doesn't make anyone important;
> sex doesn't cure problems;
> sex is not nurture; and
> sex is not insurance against abandonment,
> even if you're terrific in bed.

Crap.

To recover from shame we need to tell someone our secrets, to unburden ourselves from thinking we are the only ones who have done a particular behavior. In the 1980s I participated in a new age seminar where we all did an exercise around shame. I was in a room of two hundred people, and we all wrote down on a piece of scrap paper the one most profound shame event we still held onto. They collected all the answers, mixed them up, and passed them out to everyone. We wouldn't be reading *our* secret, and the purpose was that we would recognize that we are not alone. Most of the secrets were around sexual behavior. Numerous people had slept with cousins or relatives and felt like horrible people because of it. Some people felt ashamed because of their intimate relationship with an object and things they did when alone. We all got a big laugh of release when a seventy-five-year-old woman read, "I slept with my German shepherd." We needed a judgment-free zone to heal.

There was a sense of relief after this exercise. We all experienced a connection to one another, and none of us had to carry our shame alone. We also felt an acceptance of the complexity of the human condition. We could experience some freedom with our relationships to sex and witness our sorrow that one act can fill a body with shame that lasts forever. The only prison we stay in because of shame is our own. The idea is to be able to move through the shame and shine some light on it. We don't have to be serving penance forever.

There is nothing you have done that is worth restricting your body, heart, and mind forever locked in shame. I have had to forgive myself for endless behaviors I've participated in over the years, many not mentioned in this book. I get it. The point of this book is freedom. Freedom to love yourself no matter what. Freedom to forgive yourself no matter what. If we are stuck in shame and paralyzed by our past, we cannot be a vehicle for change and contribution.

We want to be available and present in all our relationships. Shame will hold you down, lock you in, and keep you quiet. Time to speak up and set yourself free.

Tips for Working with Shame

- Talk to someone. You are not the only one. Make sure it is someone you can trust.

- Sometimes after we share something shameful, we have residual feelings that arise in the following few days or weeks. Be aware that when we unburden ourselves, often all the reasons and fears around why we kept it secret will rise and bubble to the surface.

- Be gentle with yourself. Watch for those old ways of thinking that want to beat you up for speaking the unspeakable. Forgive, forgive, forgive.

- Recognize that we are all doing exactly what we are

capable of at any given moment. If the shame feels overwhelming, use any or all of the tools to deal with feelings: distraction, reach out to someone, journaling, exercise, etc.

- Write down five things that your best friend would say about you.

- Find a support group of some kind so you don't have to feel alone with your shame, or find a therapist who can validate your reality.

- You've got this.

Questions to Dive Deeper

1. Are there situations or events from the past that you are still feeling shame about? Are you feeling shame just for being who you are or expressing what you need or what you want?

2. What do you need to forgive yourself or others for?

3. How can you create a new belief system around who you *really* are, rather than the belief that something is wrong with you or that you are forever damaged and broken? Example: "I'm a courageous warrior who has survived feeling this way for a long time, it is no longer acceptable for me to believe this lie. I will treat myself with kindness and compassion and no longer abuse myself. We are retraining years of negative thinking. Patience.

4. What are some tools you can use to have more acceptance and compassion with yourself? Think of a daily practice that would help.

HEALING BEYOND CRAZY: Crazy Beauty

"There is also tremendous joy, beauty, love and peace within you. But they are on the other side of the pain. On the other side of the pain is ecstasy. On the other side of the pain is freedom."

—Michael Singer, *The Untethered Soul*

22

Life Is One Big Interpretation

When I was in my early 30s I was in a personal growth seminar (of course) and the leader read a quote: "You can interpret any event in your life as something that will empower you or disempower you—you choose." I've always been someone with a positive attitude, no matter what has happened to me. My mother said many times over the years that our sense of humor is the most important thing, so embrace the irony of life. It helps create a lightness, an acceptance, an engagement and a surrender to life. It helps to see things happening with a sense of spaciousness and nonattachment. Not that I don't care. I care deeply about people, but I also know what is happening all around me isn't personal. How can I be of service right now?

I remember an incest survivor I worked with years ago who was trying to figure out her relationship with God. She said, "I get the concept that we are all here to learn lessons so we can help others, but did I need the fourth violation from my father or the second rape?" I don't have an answer for that. She had to figure out how to make meaning of the events in her life and decide if she wanted to have a relationship with some kind of higher power. A power who would love, support, and accept her and be kind and tender and listen. We can all create whatever we want to believe in—that's our choice too. I choose to believe in a loving, gentle, kind, spiritual energy with a wicked sense of humor and an enormous heart because many things happen in this world that break us in two, from countries to communities, to groups, and ultimately ourselves.

Accepting things as happening with no judgment or interpretation isn't about denial or avoidance or fantasy, it is attempting to make sense of our world in a way that empowers you. The problem can be that when things are painful, it's hard to see the growth opportunity in that moment. It is after a horrendous experience has passed that we typically can recognize or illuminate or try to make sense of the *why*. We want to assimilate it into our beings rather than be broken by it. We grow up a bit. We have learned something about ourselves, we have surrendered more, or we've released more and deepened more into our truths about who we are. Sometimes the why isn't even important, it just sends us down an endless obsession for answers we don't get to find.

I turned sixty last year and it was a complete liberation. It was a wonderful birthday. I had long thick strawberry blonde hair that drove me crazy but people would say, "You have such beautiful hair" so I felt bad that I wanted to cut it. But after sixty I thought, *Are you seriously still going to be driven by what other people think!?* I had my hair cut into a pixie and I love it.

But I also noticed my interpretations, and my mind started to make stuff up about my hair. Suddenly, I felt like less of a woman or less attractive, or I told myself I shouldn't have been rebellious. I know these are just thoughts, but I was surprised by the thinking that was lying in my unconscious about hair. I want freedom. Freedom from cultural expectations, freedom from the imprisonment of what it means to be female, freedom from my underlying beliefs and shame that come forward when I do something just for me.

I lived my early life based on one major interpretation: I wasn't wanted. This was due to feeling like my mother loved my brothers but regretted having a girl because she didn't seem to like me. It launched me into a trajectory of behavior and events that led to deep shame.

When I was in graduate school in California, my mother came to visit me. We went to dinner at the Hotel Del Coronado and sat in this vast dining room of gold and red, and my mother looked so small. We talked about the struggles we had in our relationship and she told me she had always wanted to be a psychologist but she knew she had to "find a husband and have children." She said she had no regrets about her life, (meanwhile, she was drunk for most of it, just sayin') and at that moment I realized that I was living my mother's dream. I was a psychologist and I was sober.

She also said to me, "I didn't know what to do with a girl." She was admitting to me that she didn't know how to be with girls because she had grown up with brothers too. She didn't feel wanted by her own alcoholic mother, who was rigid and never wore a pair of pants in her life. She wasn't trying to reject me. She wanted me, she just didn't know how to be with me. As we say in recovery, "It's not about me." My mother and I were both the same person and completely different.

When I look back at my life, I can interpret it in a number of ways. I can be a victim/warrior, better than/less than, brilliant/reckless, didn't learn anything or learned everything. I could get in to endless comparison games that go on all over the internet, but this takes me nowhere. This is my interpretation of how life has been so far: beautiful, painful, joyous, heart breaking, adventurous, hilarious, gut-wrenching, blissful, and tragic. There have been endless opportunities to choose who I want to be. It has been a beautiful life so far and will be a beautiful life until the end. This is my choice and my interpretation. Life is all interpretation, so choose well.

Tips to Create a New Interpretation

- Begin to recognize interpretations you have made about who you are because of things that have happened in your past.

- Decide whether you want to live in these lies you have told yourself.

- Look at which beliefs empower or disempower you. Create a new interpretation. Your beliefs are only true if you decide they are.

Questions to Dive Deeper

1. Disempowering ourselves can be like an illness, a racket. It creates a false identity to try to get some need met instead of owning our true power. In can be scarier to choose our lives rather than continually sacrifice it for others. Can someone say co-crazy? What do you get out of this racket? (Ouch, I know. Breathe.)

2. Now what? Who do you want to be now?

Unreasonable vs. Unrealistic Expectations

I'm sure many of you have heard the expression "expectations are a resentment waiting to happen." It can change your life when you can see expectations from a different angle so you are not thwarted when they aren't fulfilled. This distinction of what is an unreasonable expectation and what is an unrealistic expectation can change your perception from being a victim to being a warrior. This new way of looking at things may be hard to swallow, but think about which interpretations work and empower you and which do not.

Let's use the example of my relationship to my mother. Is it unreasonable of me to expect that my mother would be a good mother, loving and kind, emotionally available, and supportive to me? No, absolutely not unreasonable. Is it *unrealistic* to think my mother would be a good mother, loving and kind, emotionally available, and supportive of me? Absolutely. My mother was fun-loving and kind but was also a detached, angry, tortured alcoholic living in an abusive relationship and raising five children. It is absolutely, completely unrealistic to expect this woman to do her job based on her history, her trauma, her circumstances, and her myriad of problems.

If I have expectations of anybody behaving in any way other

than how they are capable of behaving, it is an unrealistic expectation. Breathe. This is the thing to remember here: it does not mean I don't have power in the relationship, it doesn't mean I'm going to settle for less, it doesn't mean I have to tolerate bullshit. What it does mean is that it is up to me to find peace in that relationship, regardless of what "they are doing" or how "they are behaving." Avoiding co-crazy can occur when my happiness is not in someone else's hands, remember?

If I continue to expect my mother to be available year after year when she has not gotten sober and has not changed one bit, then whose problem is it? Why would my mother be any different if she hasn't done anything to change? In fact, most likely she will get worse because we know alcoholism and addictions are progressive illnesses. She will get worse, guaranteed. If I have called my mother after seven at night for six months and she is drunk every time, why would I continue to call her after seven? Fantasyland.

It is now my job to figure out what kind of relationship I want with my mother. I can decide not to call her at night. I could visit her on Saturday mornings or plan time with her when I know she won't be drinking. I do not put myself in a no-win situation or stay in denial about her abilities and continue to repeat my same behavior. Now I am expecting her to be different than who *she is!* If I want happiness, peace, serenity, joy, and relationships that are satisfying, I will not expect someone to be, say, or do anything that they are not capable of. Period. This is the path to freedom.

Working on ridding ourselves of those unrealistic expectations of others helps us to live in the present moment and keep the focus on ourselves. We are responsible for our behavior, thoughts, and feelings. It would be great if everyone around us behaved in the ways we want them to, but that's not how life works. People are in their own movie, living out their own drama, and their movie doesn't have anything to do with us. We can live with numerous inner agendas and expectations for the people around us, thinking they should be and act in ways that we think are right for them, but it is their life. They aren't acting in our play—they are the stars of their own. When we are trying to change, fix, help, save, or rescue another human being, it is about our inability to accept who they are being at that moment. Stay in your own movie.

Be Grateful

When I first got sober, expressing gratitude was critical to *staying* sober. Gratitude helps mitigate depression, loneliness, sadness, and grief. It helps us change our perspective from seeing the world through a dark lens, feeling consumed by self-pity, helplessness, fear, anger, comparison, and deprivation, to one of appreciation, hope, love, presence, and thankfulness. It goes back to the both/and concept. Some things have been hard and difficult and painful. *And,* there are also many, many things to be grateful for. Things always could have been worse and I feel lucky every day.

Right now, with the coronavirus going on, I feel lucky. How can this be? I work on gratitude. I work on keeping a positive perspective. I decide that I can be grateful for all that's happened rather than be stuck in regret, remorse, shame, and conflict. What are the things I have control over? What do I not have control over? I can control my own behavior, my own beliefs and actions, but I cannot control whether someone wears a mask. I am not going to give my peace and power away to a person with a different belief system. I can learn to appreciate all the good that is happening, all the service from the kindness of my fellow humans, and all of the positive change that will come from the crisis. I move into action, structuring and creating my days to be as fulfilling as possible for myself and others.

I can control my attitude, my reaction, my interpretation, my focus, and whether I fight and resist what is happening. I can surrender and embrace change and uncertainty. I can stay away from creating more drama. I can stick to the facts. This is not to say it doesn't suck at times. It is not to say some horrible things aren't happening around us—I'm not denying that. Simultaneously, it is not helpful to get caught up in the intensity of what is happening to others. Again, it's most helpful to ask yourself, *Where can I be of service?*

At night, when I get into bed, I make sure to assess all the things I *did* do in the day, not just the things I couldn't do. Do you think your perspective would change about yourself if you reviewed what you accomplished rather than just what you didn't do? Do you think your perspective would change if you thought about all the wonderful things to be grateful for, even if it is just that you are safe, you're sober, you're alive, your cat is sitting with you, you're reading a great book, and you have caramel fudge ice cream in the freezer? Sometimes that is a great day, no matter what else has happened. Be grateful. Don't deny, don't pretend, but think about what you are lucky to have, be, and do.

See the Beauty

This has been my mantra as of late. No matter what else is going on in the world, take the time to see beauty. I listened to a man on a Zoom meeting last night discuss all the things that had been going on in his life, and yet he could still notice beauty. This is an expression of gratitude and an acceptance of what is. His best friend had died in a car accident a month ago, all of his kids had moved in with him during the coronavirus pandemic and numerous circumstances in his life were very challenging, but during it all he said, "I feel peace and see the beauty of things outside my window." Yes and yes. Notice what is around you.

I'm someone who rushed through my life for years. Eventually I realized that I was missing what was right in front of me. Stop. Listen. Appreciate. I am learning to slow down and notice, take a breath, experience each moment, and be where my feet are—even if it is uncomfortable. Pause, pray, and proceed. There is such beauty surrounding us—even with protests going on everywhere, disruption, discomfort, rage, and change . . . that's beautiful. There is beauty in new voices, new openings to conversations, new awareness, and in the pain and despair it takes for these changes to take place. I will become a better person because of all this. Struggle cracks my heart open more and more each time.

Every day I see beauty in my son's big smile, the look on my crazy cat's face when he sits on my chest with his paws on my shoulders and stares at me, the brilliant colors of the flowers that I attempt to grow year after year, the doe and her baby that arrive every spring in my yard, the smell of lemon bergamot soap, listening to a David Gray album I haven't heard for a while, the tears of my friends when they get vulnerable, and the strange new wrinkles that show up on my face. Beauty is everywhere. Take a pause and notice.

Stay Open and Be Fierce—No Matter What

There are many events or opportunities in our lives where we can make a choice to shut down with pain and grief, stay angry, or stay open. Many times when something painful happens, we don't even realize we have shut our hearts down. It can also happen unconsciously to protect ourselves from future hurts. The problem is that when we shut ourselves down, we not only begin to feel less pain, but less joy as well. Shutting ourselves off from people and God is a painful place to be, so we don't want to stay there forever.

There is a great story I heard once about surrendering to "what is" and staying open no matter what happens. You can believe it or not, and the interpretation is up to you.

There was a woman who decided to stay for the weekend in New York after a business conference the previous week. Late Friday afternoon when she was returning to her hotel in a cab, she was stuck in a traffic jam while it poured rain. She was exhausted from the conference and just wanted to get back to the hotel. While the cab inched its way along with the pounding of rain on the roof, she looked out the window and there was a man coming out of a Starbucks opening an umbrella and heading toward her hotel. She thought she recognized him as a guy who was in one of her classes in graduate school and impulsively hopped out of the cab and ran up to him.

"James, is that you?"

The man turned around. It wasn't James, but it was this beautiful, dark haired, brown-eyed, stunning man who looked at her with a hint of a smile. He said, "I'm not James, but you're getting soaking wet. Where are you headed?" She pointed to the hotel, and they both jogged to the entrance while he held the umbrella over her head and touched her elbow, kindly guiding her up the stairs to the entrance.

As they shook off the wetness, the man asked, "Would you like to have a drink in the bar and dry off?" What proceeded was what she described as "the most amazing night of my life." They went to the bar and drank cognac and coffee to warm up. Then they ordered some wine, and as the conversation lingered on, they decided to have dinner together. This person that she randomly met on the streets of New York was the most interesting, brilliant, thoughtful, kind, mesmerizing, sexy, stimulating man she had encountered in her thirty-five years on the planet. She felt a connection that she had not felt previously to any other man, and she thought, *Maybe this is it, maybe this is him.*

After the food and too much wine they ended up in her hotel room for what was described as "a magical experience." He knew things about a woman's body that she didn't even know existed, and she felt passion and love and excitement and connection and bliss. She lay in his arms in the early hours of the morning thinking, *I never want this to stop. I never want this feeling to go away.* She told herself that she had found happiness once and for all. She fell asleep with beautiful memories of bodies tangled together and beautiful brown eyes that she felt looked into her soul.

When she woke up in the morning he was gone. She looked around the room and in the bathroom and there was no evidence of him being there and no note. She was devastated. *How could I have the most meaningful, magical evening of my life and have it vanish in a split second? This can't be happening.* She called her best friend, Stuart, whom she had known since childhood, and told him the entire story and sobbed. After venting for half an hour and letting the tears flow, she said, "What do I do?" Stuart paused and said, "Pray for more rain?"

No matter what happens, no matter how many times our hearts have been broken—and there will be many—stay open. Keep the loving heart open, no matter what. Be fierce. We can move through pain and broken hearts and losses and people passing through our lives. We can thrive and forgive and keep loving—just keep loving—because that is what this journey is all about.

Leaving Crazy Town

Clean up Your Life—Especially Your Relationships

If we are choosing to live in a way that doesn't match up to our values, we are not going to feel good about it. This next suggestion isn't about perfectionism, it's about beginning to change behaviors to line them up with the vision of ourselves.

Due to my journey to recovery from addiction and co-crazy, I feel complete and clear with most people from my past and present. There is not much left unsaid. We realize in recovery that if we have done things we feel bad about, or left something unsaid, there is an energy that holds our lives down. Whether it is guilt or remorse or regret or fear that has gotten in our way of cleaning up these relationships, it is time now to take action. If we've done things that we need to apologize for, just do it. If we have not told someone we love them because we are afraid, just do it. We need to consider others before we take these risks, but carrying around energy from the past is not going to lead to freedom. For example, it took me a long time to make amends to my mother.

Unfortunately, it happened after she died, and I had to do a graveside amend. I behaved in ways I regretted and must have hurt her deeply. She had an illness that was not her fault, and she did the best she could. Over time I was able to see my life from my mother's point of view and how painful it must have been for her. I have incredible compassion for her now. I am only responsible for the things I did, and I needed to make it right. At times I still acknowledge my feelings of regret over my behaviors. Some things we can't make better, but we can learn to live with them as we create new behaviors that bring harmony, not destruction.

We can only clean up things we are able to. We also can't make anyone accept our apology. We can only do our part, and we aren't responsible for how people respond to us. When I was married to Shane, I saw myself as a victim. When I began to do some of my amend work, I did not think I needed to apologize to Shane for anything. I had been with him for seven years! Do you think it is possible that I may have done one thing to hurt him? When I worked through my anger toward him and grief about the marriage, I was able to see more clearly what part I played in our conflicts. I did end up sitting down with him and apologizing for many things that were not okay. He is one of my challenges, even today, but we clean up our relationship regularly, sweeping off our sides of the street. Neither of us wants to hold on to past energy that can get in the way of us living fully today.

Leaving Crazy Town

Be Vulnerable: Look at the Ways You Stay Distant from People

This suggestion is easier said than done, but it is the true way to intimacy. When we can allow ourselves to be vulnerable and tell the truth, we experience a real connection. It takes time to figure out how to express our authentic selves. If we look at our lives and see a lack of intimate relationships, then we may become aware that we resist vulnerability and have a need to feel in control. It can be lonely when we're hiding out and we don't feel safe enough to share our real thoughts and feelings. I am so grateful for the experience of knowing there are people on this planet who get me, but I still struggle with being vulnerable. We all need to embrace our needy parts. Yuck.

As I grew and changed over time in my recovery, my relationships changed. We have some people who will be our friends forever. They are our soul sisters and brothers. There are others in our lives for a reason or a season or a lesson to be learned. My son was four years old when Rob entered my life. Before he relapsed, he taught me so much about intimacy, boundaries, trusting God, and honoring our true selves. His lessons have lasted until now, and they have forever changed me. I will always be grateful to him for that. I've had to allow my heart to open gradually and my armor to fall and clang on the ground, but it has been a slow process. The most rewarding, fulfilling connections I have had over the years happened when I allowed myself to be vulnerable, truthful, and open.

We all have aspects of our personality that we think are "just my personality" but they really are ways we try to stay safe. They are developed from an early hypervigilance to survive. They do the opposite of what we want, which is to feel connected. These are ways of operating that we developed to try to get what we wanted or needed if we couldn't feel safe enough to ask. They can become long-standing behavior traits or characteristics that were created early in life to get our needs met but they no longer serve us as adults.

These are some of the ways we stay in this image, protection, and identity, rather than explore all the parts of our personalities and trust that we can meet our own needs now. Try a different technique. Try to go through a day without complaining. Go through a day where you pause and count to ten every time you feel angry. If you are permanently nice (afraid to upset people), try telling someone the truth. Notice how you feel when you just ask for what you want and don't try to manipulate a situation. These are all ways to try to expand who you are and not be so stuck in a false identity. Trying a new behavior will help you see what fears are underneath that are stopping you, and help you gain the freedom to be who you want to be.

Leaving Crazy Town

Take Back Your Body

For many people with addiction issues or co-crazy behaviors, we find it difficult to be present in our bodies experiencing all that our bodies feel. For addicts, we spend our lives trying to escape what we are feeling, thinking, and physically experiencing, so we use anything to find relief from whatever pain we are avoiding. For co-crazy people, we spend too much time in our heads creating scenarios about what is right for this person or that person, not even realizing we are emotionally taking up someone else's space rather than experiencing our own.

For years, I didn't even realize I wasn't feeling what was happening in my body. Whether it was discomfort about another's behavior or a chronic tension of anxiety to avoid my feelings, I was detached from my own physical experience. It has taken years of practicing mindfulness, somatic therapies, yoga, and other forms of breath work and exercise to be in my body and feel fully connected to it. I had been holding past trauma, memories, experiences, and feelings throughout my body not knowing that it was affecting me physically by creating chronic stomach problems, unceasing fatigue, and relentless neck tension. Until I felt safe enough to actually experience all that my body was experiencing, I couldn't feel fully integrated. I'm still a work in progress.

This may sound crazy to people. Of course you feel your body, right? Not necessarily. Right now, think about where your shoulders are, where your feet are; are you hungry, are you angry, are you tired? Take a moment just to be present in your body. What does it feel like? I had no idea how much time I spent *not* experiencing my bodily sensations. If we want to live fully and experience our lives in a joyful, present way, we want to begin to embrace the space our bodies take up and all its sensations.

For years I was ashamed of my body. I was controlled and preoccupied by thoughts of: I was too big, my hair was the wrong color, my legs were too short, my eyes were too small, my breasts were too big, and my face was too round. As women, we never seem to feel like we are enough. Thin enough, smart enough, funny enough, beautiful enough, enough, enough. My body was not enough. The desire to escape this beautiful soul carrier began as a young girl with that first belief comparing myself to all my brothers with the conclusion that I'm not them; therefore, I'm not enough. I'm not right. Something is wrong with me. I needed out.

So come back to that body, that beautiful piece of human flesh that has held your heart and guarded your soul. Know that feelings are just feelings, clouds passing by. There is a beginning, a middle, and an end to them. They don't last forever. Know that you will never die from a feeling, only the behaviors you use to avoid them. Be proud of your strength, your wounds, your marks of history that cover your skin with scars and brown spots and cellulite and tattoos and wrinkles. I needed to carry it like it meant something, like I cared about it, like it's the only one I've got, like it has saved me from battles of love to tears of joy and release.

I continue to lighten that load of history and heal the fatigue in my muscles and bones from fighting something I needed to just surrender to. *What is.* That's it. Just surrender to what is, not resisting, not holding up the shield and covering myself with a panoply, just surrender and release, accept and release, love it and release. Instead of holding on anymore to the past, or resisting what comes in the present, or cowering fearfully in darkness from what the future may bring, just sit in the sunlight and feel the warmth of the spirit to heal it all.

Move your body as much as possible so you can feel its strength. I decided a long time ago I didn't need to *like* exercising or pushing myself physically, I just needed to do it. What liberation. I was always waiting until I *felt* like it and it would never happen. What I know is I feel much better when I'm exercising and moving regularly. Even when sometimes I only have the energy for walking a few times a week. It is a time right now in the culture where we do a lot of sitting, and experts say it is one of the worst things for us, that we need to try to move at least ten minutes for every hour. This isn't about perfection, just make small changes to start moving.

I also recommend body therapies. There are different kinds of therapies that work with how we hold our past events locked within our bodies, leading to chronic tension and somatic complaints. I have had amazing experiences participating in some of these therapies to release frozen wounds from the past. We can intellectualize a hurt, but often we can't release it from our system physiologically. Due to past trauma (not necessarily a huge event like war or sexual abuse), our bodies get permanently stuck in fight, flight, or freeze. If you are having body symptoms that are hard to figure out, you may think of utilizing some tools from the somatic therapy world.

Get present in your body. Learn to honor it, listen to it, embrace it, feel it. Be grateful for what you have rather than being in the perseverative thinking of wishing it were different. Own it. Appreciate it. It's brought you this far.

23

Finding Freedom

When I had breast cancer in 2017, I would drive to the hospital early in the morning and receive radiation and then go to work. One morning I was driving down Route 2 in Concord, MA, blasting the Rolling Stones' "Gimme Shelter," and I had this realization that I would rather be going to a radiation treatment than going to work. Uh oh. Who said that?

That moment was when I realized that it took getting cancer to see that I was burned out, fried, depleted, and exhausted. I was not functioning at my best. For three years or so, I had been talking to friends about transitioning to something different. The problem is I love what I do. I love helping people. I love addicts and alcoholics, and they have saved my life as much as I have saved theirs. I was afraid of change, afraid of the unknown, afraid to rest—not to mention, what about health insurance? But at that moment I knew I needed to save my life once again and stop.

I had been taking in people's pain for too long. My body felt like the cartoon of an old box computer where the systems have all shut down and there is smoke coming out the top and wires hanging off the sides with cracks on every surface. My system was down. I had known it for a while but didn't want to acknowledge it. Work was my joy, my purpose, my calling, my worth, and I lived by George Bernard Shaw's quote about the splendid torch. It says, "I want to be thoroughly used up when I die, for the harder I work the more I live. I rejoice in life for its own sake. Life is no brief candle for me. It is a sort of splendid torch which I have got hold of for the moment, and I want to make it burn as brightly as possible before handing it on to future generations." The trouble was that my fire was extinguishing, my light was only a flicker, and my spirit was laying on her back on the floor saying, "Help."

I've listened to people do horrible things to themselves and their families. People hurting others, being hurt, or wanting someone to hurt them. People dying from drug addiction, alcoholism, sex addiction, risky behaviors, chronic illnesses, and broken hearts. I've witnessed the discomfort and pain and beauty of someone finally setting a limit and begin to care of themselves. I've also witnessed many, many, many people get clean and sober, heal their hearts, find their spirits, and soar. This is the gift of working with addicts. Many therapists have said to me over the years, "It is hard to know if we are really making a difference." I do understand that; however, when you work with addicts and they put the substances down, you get to watch their lives take off to the stars. I get to witness miracles.

I've watched the crazy beauty of people coming back to themselves after years of being lost in the "incomprehensible demoralization" of addiction, or the chronic anxiety and depression of co-crazy. I have seen people's lives transform from a woman being in a twenty-year domestic violence relationship to celebrating ten years of sobriety and freedom. The pendulum swings from my stomach wrenching one day while hearing a woman describe dropping her baby while breast feeding because she was drunk, to feeling elation hearing about a client celebrating getting her graduate degree to become a therapist after five years of sobriety. This is life. All of it. Every single rich, beautiful, tragic, wonderful, heartbreaking part of it.

A mentor of mine once said that working with addicts is like working on a cancer ward. Lots of people die. If you have been around the recovery world long enough you will hear

244 Sarah Michaud, PsyD

about many tragic endings. Addiction is lethal and dangerous and insane and reckless and painful and ruins lives and families. One of my closest friends described his heroin use like kissing God, so no wonder we're f**ked. Over the years I've known many people who didn't make it. Dan jumped in front of a train, John overdosed on heroin, Doug was found dead in the old Combat Zone in Boston after a night with strippers, Debra jumped off of a building, Jesse slit her own throat. There are also many who survive from self-inflicted wounds on their wrists, thighs, even gunshots to the face, it happens.

We are warriors—every single one of us who has survived addiction, lived with addiction, felt addiction, grown up with addiction, or married addiction. It hurts like no other hurt. The loss of life, the loss of relationships, the twisted minds of our children thinking that we don't love them because we chose alcohol—whatever it is. It's awful, it's unbearable, it's heart-breaking, and I hate being powerless over others' addictions. I hate it. I also know how powerful our behaviors can be to help someone face themselves more quickly or choose sobriety and even choose life.

Co-crazy or just plain crazy. I have felt both and often. I've been an addict, I grew up in addiction, I've worked with addicts, sponsored addicts, been married to addicts, and most of my friends are addicts. As I said at the beginning of this book, *they are everywhere*. They are your neighbors, your boss, your lover, your child, your teacher, and even your gynecologist. (I ran in to my gyno at an AA meeting. Awkward.) I'm not great with statistics, but I do know the world is deeply affected by the loss of human souls to the addiction to drugs and alcohol. As well as lives lost to the addiction to another human being who they think they can change. Both are lethal.

This co-crazy dance is caused by the love we have for people with addictions or other struggles. The dance of powerlessness/action, insanity/sanity, stillness/chaos, control/surrender, letting go/holding on. Life and death. We are healing from the dance of co-crazy and the dance within ourselves to find the truth so we can choose life. Step off the dance floor and choose you.

The ultimate goal for me was freedom from the chains of addiction. Freedom from the crazy in relationships. Freedom from feeling responsible for other people's lives and happiness. Freedom from chronic fear and resentment. Freedom to do what was right for me. Freedom to set boundaries and make healthy choices. Freedom from living in secrets and shame. Freedom to allow my true self to come forward and be okay with that person, no matter what. Freedom to be vulnerable. Freedom to find my voice. I'm getting there.

After I asked Rob to move out, I was in rough shape. I knew I needed to get out of myself, find some friends, get back into therapy, and start making some changes. I got active in my twelve-step programs again, tried some new meetings, and became committed to working through my co-crazy. During this time, a sponsee of mine from ten years before resurfaced in my life. She reached out to me because she was going through a horrendous breakup and her heart had been crushed. We began to spend time together, and I became her sponsor again. She thought I was saving her life, but she was saving mine.

This idea of how helping others helps ourselves always amazes me. Real support, not co-crazy. Helping others gets me out of myself when I'm feeling blue and I've lost perspective. When we are in a self-centered spiral of pain, fear and hurt, getting a broader perspective always helps. Helping my friend through her heartache and breakup helped me to get perspective on my own situation. She helped me to see how much there is to be grateful for and to remember that things do pass. Often, when we are in self-pity, getting that gratitude list filled up changes our attitude and gives us an appreciation for life.

When I left Rob, Max was in fifth grade. He is now at college and creating his own life. What is guaranteed is that more change is ahead for both of us. I am so proud of this young man. I often say we learn the most about ourselves through our parenting. He has helped me become the person I am and heal parts of myself I never knew were still operating. Parenting is one of the biggest gifts and the biggest challenges to do well.

At times, to not react to some of the things our kids say takes a miracle and feels like divine intervention.

Knowing in my heart of hearts that I did not want to repeat the patterns of my parents, I worked hard at being a good parent, but we all make plenty of mistakes. Shane is still in my life and will be forever. He is my son's dad. We believe we are working out some past karma with each other. The good news is that we don't hurt each other—we are honest and try to be supportive of one another.

I still have a small private practice, but I've cut down over the last few years. After the moment on the highway going to my radiation appointment, I took an online burnout quiz, and I scored off the charts. At the end of the test, these big red letters were flashing "Danger Zone" and I thought, *Okay, Sarah, maybe it's time to do something else.* I've truly loved working with clients. They have taught me about compassion, resilience, and the human spirit. They have cracked my heart open, shared their vulnerabilities, and showed me the courage of gladiators. They have all been a blessing. I love them all.

When Rob first moved out after his relapse, he made several attempts to get sober again. He moved in with his daughter but she ended up asking him to leave when he kept using. He felt the endless losses that happen with addiction resurfacing and eventually ended up in a "wet" shelter where you can stay even if you are still drinking. When I met Rob, he had his own business, had been sober for many years, had many friends, sponsored people, and his nickname was Spiritual Rob. Within nine months of my asking him to leave, he was barely surviving. A year or so later, he made it to a long-term treatment facility for veterans. We tried to make our marriage work. I would visit him and we'd go on walks, or go to a beach just to sit and try to connect again. But the truth was he wasn't ever the same and neither was I. My own truth was that I couldn't trust him and I couldn't go back. His truth was that he could not get back his sobriety.

In this halfway house, most of the guys were still using drugs or pills and were not involved in any recovery program. Rob had a lot of shame about what had happened and how far down he had gone again. He had lost everything. That is not to say people can't come back from a relapse because I've seen it happen all the time. Rob couldn't do it. I eventually realized I needed to let him go.

A few years ago, I was in a meeting and my phone started buzzing. It was Rob's son. The minute I saw who was calling, I knew Rob had died. I called his son back, and we talked for a while. I hadn't seen his children in a couple of years. Rob had been found in his apartment after being dead for a few days. Addiction at its finest: devastating endings for beautiful human beings.

Right now, I'm in a peaceful place. I'm excited about the changes coming, and I'm trying to appreciate every moment. I'm looking at what brings me joy, staying open to the journey ahead, enjoying all I have, and nurturing my relationship with my God. I continue to do my life and recovery maintenance. I wrote this book because I wanted to spread the message of recovery. Not just recovery from addiction, but also recovery from relationship insanity. Relationships can be a source of incredible conflict and deep pain, or they can be blissful and the most beautiful aspect of our lives.

I am sharing everything I've learned so far that has worked for me. I want to spread the message that addiction and co-crazy can happen to anyone. As a psychologist who has done her best in her recovery, I still got slammed by co-crazy behaviors even after I made great strides away from old patterns. Take what you like and leave the rest. These are only suggestions. I know how painful it can be when you are struggling and feeling crazy in a relationship, and how difficult it is to stay focused on your own life. The Buddhist author Pema Chödrön says, *"The truth is not convenient."* We often do not want to face the truth. We have that right. My hope is that this book brought you some peace, a new beginning, and a moment of hope that things can be different.

Healing co-crazy is like coming home to our true selves who have always been there. It requires self-love, patience, courage, acceptance, kindness, compassion, and a willingness to save our own lives. Ongoingly as we practice new skills, we will feel more open, expressive, grounded, free, and less angry and anxious. We will find peace in our hearts as we stand in love with the true essence of our being. We will be unwilling to sacrifice our beauty and power for anything or anyone.

Note to Readers

Taking Addictive Substances in Recovery

Over the almost forty years I've been in recovery, I have taken pain medications for different medical issues. While in recovery, taking an addictive substance can be complex and even deadly. This decision requires input from health professionals and trusted confidants. The most important part of making this decision is making sure you do *not* do it alone. Don't attempt to manage pain or another psychological or medical issue in shame and silence.

Truth and addiction repel each other. The trouble is that addicts can be full of shit, and we can lie to ourselves and others when we are ashamed, want relief or just want to use again. If you are considering taking an addictive substance and you are in recovery, make sure somebody else knows—someone who you can't bullshit, someone who's got your back, someone who isn't Co-crazy.

Big love,

Sarah

About the Author

Dr. Sarah Michaud PsyD is a clinical psychologist with a private practice in Central Massachusetts. For over thirty years her main field of practice has been helping families and individuals recover from drug and alcohol addiction as well as from the many unhealthy co-dependencies that occur. She completed her doctorate program at the California School of Professional Psychology (San Diego), then moved back to Boston to work at a well-known psychiatric hospital, where she helped to open a residential program for dually diagnosed clients. Sarah's unique position as an authority in the field is also due to growing up in an alcoholic household, becoming addicted to alcohol and cocaine, and marrying two addicts in recovery. Her own struggle into recovery from addiction and relationship insanity is an inspiration for all readers.

As Michaud says, "I lost myself and found myself many times—hopefully to be solid enough now to not get lost again or at least find my way back more quickly." *Co-Crazy* provides clear, attainable, no-nonsense advice for millions of families who have suffered the human cost of addiction and codependency. The author lives outside of Boston.

For more information please visit *www.drsarahmichaud.com.*

Acknowledgments

My first acknowledgement goes to the writing team of Bradley Cooper and Lady Gaga's characters in the movie *A Star Is Born*.

There is a scene in the movie where the two characters, Jack and Ally, are talking about talent and that everyone has something to say. He impresses on her to have the courage to put herself out there because *she* has something to say . . . even though she didn't like it. After watching this scene in the movie, it gave me the courage to think I had something to say and to finally get the courage to say it (even though I didn't like it). Thank you to all involved in the film for showing us the beautiful and heartbreaking truth of addiction and co-crazy.

To Lisa Akoury-Ross at SDP Publishing and Highline Editorial, New York, for believing in me and giving me endless encouragement. You have no idea how much it helped to read all your kind words.

To my best pals Susan and Linda:

Susan, you are a true warrior princess. Thank you for all the love, support, kind words, endless encouragement, and hours of listening to my confusion, excitement, despair, and surrender around this book.

Linda Mac, thank you for our ongoing lunches, for talking with me about manifesting our bountiful lives, the belly laughs, the looks of confusion on your face, the ongoing commentary about what God's plan is for us (or so we thought), and the realization that the "ten million" had been here all along.

To my writing group, where it all started in the fall of 2018, where you gave me permission to write. Thanks to Anne, Paula, Marilyn, Sharon, Gail, and Lorraine.

To the warriors who make my life make sense: Beth, Finn, Norah, Mary, Sheila, Anne, Marybeth and Gretchen. To all the women in our Coming Home to Ourselves Group, thank you for giving me the opportunity to try the book out and all your loving support in encouraging me to come home to my true self: Wanda, Margit, Jane, Eileen, Maureen, Laurel, Erin, Sharlene, Suzanne and Jamie.

To my brother Broo for reading the first draft and encouraging me to "keep writing."

To my brother Stu for having my back since we were three years old. Know that I will always have yours. Thank you for being the loving, brilliant, kind, funny, open-hearted man I know. If more men were like you, the world would be a better place.

To my brothers, Davie and Johnny, for helping me survive childhood.

To all the men in my life who have taught me more about myself than they will ever know, especially my two ex-husbands.

To the most important man in my life, who has taught me how to be a better person every day and who makes me laugh relentlessly, my son Max.

To all the people in recovery meetings around the world, you save my life every single day.

To Bill W, who wrote the most magnificent book in the world, who created a solution when there was none, who has created a place for drunks like me to go and feel at home, and whose legacy continues to save lives every day, thanks for saving mine.

To Dr B, for everything.

To all my clients over the years who have opened my heart and shared their souls—it is always an honor.

To a loving God who continues to have my back no matter what.

Additional Resources

There are *many* support groups out there. I encourage you to find a group where you feel comfortable and heard.

Possibilities

Alcoholics Anonymous www.aa.org

National Helpline www.samhsa.org

Refugee Recovery www.refugerecovery.org

Al-Anon www.al-anon.org

Helpful Books

The Untethered Soul: The Journey Beyond Yourself by Michael Singer (New Harbinger Publications, 2007)

Comfortable with Uncertainty: 108 Teachings on Cultivating Fearlessness and Compassion by Pema Chödrön (Shambhala, 2002)

Daring Greatly: How the Courage to Be Vulnerable Transforms the Way We Live, Love, Parent, and Lead by Brené Brown (Avery, 2012)

10% Happier by Dan Harris (HarperCollins, 2014)

Codependent No More: How to Stop Controlling Others and Start Caring for Yourself by Melody Beattie (Hazelden, 1986)

Facing Love Addiction: Giving Yourself the Power to Change the Way You Love by Pia Melody, with Andrea Wells Miller, and J. Keith Miller (HarperOne, 1989)

The Four Agreements: A Practical Guide to Personal Freedom by Don Miguel Ruiz (Amber-Allen Publishing, 2018)

Brave Enough by Cheryl Strayed (Knopf Doubleday Publishing Group, 2015)

In an Unspoken Voice: How the Body Releases Trauma and Restores Goodness by Peter A. Levine, PhD (North Atlantic Books, 2010)

Boundaries: When to Say Yes, How to Say No To Take Control of Your Life by Henry Cloud and John Townsend (Zondervan, 2017)

Getting the Love You Want: A Guide for Couples (Third Edition) by Harville Hendrix, PhD, and Helen LaKelly Hunt, PhD (St. Martin's Griffin, 2019)

The Language of Letting Go: Daily Meditations for Codependents by Melody Beattie (Hazelden Publishing, 1990)

Women, Sex and Addiction: A Search for Love and Power by Charlotte Kasl, PhD (HarperCollins, 1990)

When the Body Says No: Exploring the Stress-Disease Connection by Gabor Maté, MD (Wiley Publishing, 2011)

The Artist's Way: A Spiritual Path to Higher Creativity (25th Anniversary Edition) by Julie Cameron (TarcherPerigee, 2016)

The Power of Now: A Guide to Spiritual Enlightenment by Eckhart Tolle (New World Library, 1999)

Breath: The New Science of a Lost Art by James Nestor (Riverhead Books, 2020)

Have a New Kid by Friday: How to Change Your Child's Attitude, Behavior, and Character in 5 Days by Dr. Kevin Leman (Revel, 2008)

Have a New Teenager by Friday: From Mouthy and Moody to Respectful and Responsible in 5 Days by Dr. Kevin Leman (Revel, 2011)

Notes

Epigraph

Scandal. 2013. Season 2, Episode 19, "Seven Fifty-Two." Directed by Allison Liddi-Brown. Aired April 25, 2013 on ABC.

Part I: A Crazy and Co-Crazy Life: Crash and Burn

Cheryl Strayed, *Brave Enough* (New York: Knopf Doubleday Publishing Group, 2015), 8.

Chapter 3

Alcoholics Anonymous (New York: Works Publishing Company, 1939), 46.

Part II: MY STORY: How Did I Catch It? The Progression of Addiction and Co-Crazy

Chapter 7

Alcoholics Anonymous (New York: Works Publishing Company, 1939), 30.

A, Peter (2019) Conversation with Peter A.

Chapter 9

Werner Erhard, "The est Standard Training" (lecture, Copley Plaza Hotel, Boston, MA, 1986).

Part III: THOSE F*ING THOUGHTS AND FEELINGS: Working With the Core of Co-Crazy**

Chapter 11

Werner Erhard, "The est Standard Training" (lecture, Copley Plaza Hotel, Boston, MA, 1986).

Alcoholics Anonymous (New York: Works Publishing Company, 1939), 64.

Chapter 12

Alcoholics Anonymous (New York: Works Publishing Company, 1939), 62.

Chapter 15

Alcoholics Anonymous (New York: Works Publishing Company, 1939), 62.

Werner Erhard, "The est Standard Training" (lecture, Copley Plaza Hotel, Boston, MA, 1986).

Part IV: RECOVERY: Jumping Off the Crazy Train

Coming Home to Ourselves codependency recovery group online Zoom meeting.

Chapter 17

Alcoholics Anonymous (New York: Works Publishing Company, 1939), 449.

Chapter 21

Charlotte Davis Kasl, PhD., *Women, Sex and Addiction: A Search for Love and Power* (New York: HarperCollins, 1989), 3.

Part V: HEALING BEYOND CRAZY: Crazy Beauty

Michael A. Singer, *The Untethered Soul: The Journey beyond Yourself* (Oakland: New Harbinger Publications, 2007), 105.

Chapter 22

Werner Erhard, "The est Standard Training" (lecture, Copley Plaza Hotel, Boston, MA, 1986).

Chapter 23

Man and Superman, written by George Bernard Shaw, dir. J Augustus Keogh, Royal Court Theatre, London, May 23 1905.

Pema Chödrön, Comfortable with Uncertainty (Berkeley: Shambala Publications, 2002), 177.

Co-Crazy

One Psychologist's Recovery from
Codependency and Addiction

A Memoir and Roadmap to Freedom

Sarah Michaud, PsyD

Publisher: SDP Publishing

Also available in ebook format

SDP Publishing

www.SDPPublishing.com

Contact us at: info@SDPPublishing.com

CPSIA information can be obtained
at www.ICGtesting.com
Printed in the USA
JSHW042319151222
34976JS00001B/7